D0288271

"On the sands lie the bleached bones of millions, who when they had victory in their grasp, hesitated and in waiting, died."
Bill France, Sr.

Sitting in the media center of the Pocono Raceway, my eyes and mind wandered to the wall where these simply framed, hand-written words were hung. They struck me as true and vitally important, not only for all drivers, but for everyone in the human "race." If there is a victory in this book, the credit goes to the people responsible for creating, pioneering, and proliferating the sport of stock car racing.

We dedicate this book to everyone who ever raced a dirt track, sacrificed to run a race, or paid the ultimate price with their life. Your courage has moved us, your tenacity has motivated us, and your faith has inspired us.

The list, far too large to enumerate for this dedication, would not be complete without mention of the people, past and present, who gave their lives to compete. To the drivers, team owners, crew, track owners, staff, journalists, film crews, photographers and, of course, to the fans, *From the Heart of Racing* dedicates this first edition to you.

ACKNOWLEDGEMENTS

I would first like to give thanks to our LORD and Savior, Jesus Christ, for offering us a life of grace and the opportunity to bring you the *Healing Voice Publishing and From the Heart of Racing*.

To my wife, Ellen, and daughters, Angelique and Sarah, for their continuous patience in allowing me to follow my vision during the long, hard days on the road and the weeks of writing, deadlines, edits, promotion and marketing. Their warm hugs and happy faces kept me focused on the goal and made it all worthwhile. Ellen's continued efforts in raising and caring for the children in my absence were critical in allowing me to focus, create, and continue. To my mother, Angela, for her constant prayers and reminders to use my head and not my heart in every decision I owe an unending debt of gratitude. Her fearless, tireless, hard work and dedication to the family served as the one role model I count on throughout my life. You are my hero, Mom.

For her support in the final edits and managing to control the unthinkable task of organizing me on the road and in the office, I would like to thank my personal assistant, Donna Swicegood. Your kindness and hard work made finishing a reality and joy. Thanks also to Margie McGraw for taking her gifts of clarity, education and experience to head up the editing and development of our work. To Jan Teel for her unlimited strength, energy and commitment to detail. For the bulk of the editing to fall on such a great writer, a super person, and a strong Christian witness we can only say "GOD Bless you!"

A very special debt of gratitude to the "G-Man," Gordon Gregory, and his company, **CDRC**, for the education and constant organizational aptitude that were absolutely essential in putting this incredible CD presentation of the Petty Family Tradition together in under three months. Your dedication has been acknowledged but the content of the project and your friendship is the real victory of the test.

FROM THE HEART OF RACING

Ron Camacho
Max Helton

A Healing Voice Publishing
A subsidiary of American Entertainment Concepts, Inc.
128 Holiday Court, Suite 116
Franklin, Tennessee

www.fromtheheartof.com/racing

I

ISBN 0-9705776-9-9
COPYRIGHT INFORMATION

©2000 Ron Camacho and Max Helton

All rights reserved. Printed in the United States of
America. No part of this publication may be
reproduced, stored in a retrieval system or
transmitted in any form or by any means, electronic,
mechanical, photocopying, recording or otherwise
without the written permission of the publisher.

A HEALING VOICE PUBLISHING
A SUBSIDIARY OF
AMERICAN ENTERTAINMENT CONCEPTS, INC.
128 HOLIDAY COURT, SUITE 116
FRANKLIN, TENNESSEE 37067

Grateful acknowledgement for permission to reprint
is made as follows: *The Book of Stock Car Wisdom*
by Criswell Freeman, Walnut Grove Press © 1996.

Many people should be credited for the production of any book. It takes time away from other very worthy projects and precious time that normally is spent with family and friends. Max Helton would like to express his gratitude to his loving and supportive family...my wife, Jean, my daughters, Elaine, Melanie Barker, Crista, and Becky Chapman...for my four grandchildren, D.J., Brooke, Samuel, and Madison, who have had to wait for Papa's trips to Dairy Queen...for my Dad and Mom, Herman and Nellie, who have patiently waited for a visit from their son...to Missy DeSouza, my personal assistant, for her work in taking care of my other work...to Billy Mauldin, the COO of MRO for his encouragement to do this project in the first place...to all of those who have shared their lives with me.

From the Heart would like to express our thanks to Bill Lardie, and Debra McKirdy, president and senior book buyer of Anderson Merchandise, and the Wal-Mart company for sharing our vision. Without their valuable contributions this exclusive edition would not have come about in the fashion and the time frame it has.

On behalf of Ron Camacho, American Entertainment Concepts Inc., The Healing Voice Publishing, and Max Helton we offer our deepest gratitude to the following people for coming around us and making the impossible, possible:

To Jim Hannigan for a supernatural belief, education, prayers and actions on our behalf. Without his dedication and the constant organization and commitment, the unbelievable task of putting together the CD from before the start of production to the permission process, the Petty Family Tradition CD simply would not have been possible. To Audra Koontz, Martha Jane Bonkemeyer, Anne Fogleman, Doris Gammons and the entire staff at Petty Enterprises, thank you for your continuous effort and support.

To the entire Petty family for the courage to allow us to represent their tradition with clarity and candor through the grievous events of this past year. This family's dignity in the face of great loss stands as a lesson to us all, of the power of faith, family and charity.

V

To the drivers, team owners, and crews - Bobby Allison, Darrell Waltrip, Dale Earnhardt, Jeff Gordon, Mark Martin, Dale Jarrett, Bobby Labonte, Dale Earnhardt, Jr., Kenny Wallace, Sterling Marlin, Joe Nemechek, Brett Bodine, Tony Stewart, Andy Santerre, Tim Fedewa, Bobby Hillian, Jr., Ernie Irvan, Bill Venturini, Jimmy Johnson, Steve Park, Buckshot Jones, Greg Davis, Barry Dodson, Chocolate Meyers, Felix Sabates--thank you for sharing your personal stories.

To Kenny Irwin, Sr. and his wife, Reva, for granting us an interview and allowing us to use Kenny's image on the cover. His story has graced this book and in sharing with us, his memory will live through its pages and in our hearts.

To the head of promotions of the Lowe's Motor Speedway, Jerry Gappens, and Retired Major General Thomas Sadler, of the Speedway Children Charities, for being among the first people to believe in our vision and support us early on. To H. A. "Humpy" Wheeler, COO, president and general manager of Lowe's Motor Speedway and Bruton Smith, CEO of SMI and their credential staff, Myra Faulkenbury and Ida Strovinger for their kindness and generosity for allowing Ron and the AMENTCO staff to attend the races over the last two years.

To our contributing writers, Chris Economacki, "The Insider"-- Claire B. Lang, Brad Winters, John Shaughnessy and the *Indianapolis Star* and Tony Johns. To Bob Latford for helping us set up our grading system for our websites. To the editor extraordinaire, Mr. Bill King. Jon Davidson, Ben Blake at *Racer Magazine* and Tom Higgins for information and inspiration. To Mike "The Snowman" Snow, for the racing and wrestling updates.

Thanks to the fans who contributed their stories to our book: Brian Spivey, Susan Santerre, Kathy Nelson, Jane Smith, Tom Mason, Tony Johns, Karen Fenrich, Kira Bloomingdale, Cheryl Walker, Jim Rosati, Margie Lambert, Ginger Wolfson, Susan Tribucher, DW from SC, Richard Rabenold, William Kirk II, Walter Mabe, Jenni Thompson, Larry Baldwin, John Whitlock and Jan Teel.

Doak Turner, senior coordinator of the NSAI, opened his condo doors for the first two years of my journey. His continuous acts of kindness were the first, and the most important, steps in helping me keep my faith up, my heart warm, and my stomach happy.

To the Carolina Marketing and the Visual Marketing Team of Randy Poyer – Dot Roper, Kurt Stiles, Bob Jankowski and "Little" Bud Moore for letting us rent the cabin behind the Charlotte Lowe's Motor Speedway for final edits. The constant support, personally and professionally made the difference in the closing months of this production.

To artist extraordinaire, Rana Robertson, Gretchen Dabney, and Jennifer Chappel of Motorsports Management Group, I can't say enough "Thank You's." David Litwin and Josh Womack for giving us our identity and web creations.

To Synergy Studios, Randy Seeds and Ken Bonham for the *From the Heart of Racing* web page and ratings system. Your contribution has been invaluable.

To track owner's and staff: Lowe's Motor Speedway, Jerry Gappens, North Carolina Speedway, Christy Richardson, Pocono Raceway, Dr. Joseph Mattioli and Dr. Rose Mattioli, Bob Pleban, Talladega Super Speedway, Rick Humphrey, and Pam Smith, Bristol Motor Speedway, Wayne Estes, Martinsville Speedway, and Dick Thompson, Atlanta Motor Speedway.

To First Tennessee Bank, a very special thank you to David Ellis, Becky Ericson, Lori Carver, Shirley Allan, and Kimberly Talbert.

Our film crews, Ross "The Boss" Bennett, George Sozio and Greg Paige, of PK Productions, and our photographers Don Hunter, Vernon Theriault, Mark Sluder and Walter Arce.

To my attorney, Orville Almon and his assistant, Karen Thomas, for taking on AMENTCO's legal work through thick and thin.

To Capitol Records and the recording artists, Stir, for their song, "Clear."

To Nealy and Jeremy Perry of Perry Shell in Nashville for their continuous support, hugs and smiles for my family -- to say nothing of the necessary fuel that kept us rolling down the NASCAR trail.

To Kathy Perry, Maureen Ritchie, Julie Keenan and the R.R. Donnelly staff.

To Lisa Webb, Rodney Aistrop, Don McIntyre, Scott Applegate, Lacy Hunter , Eva Hunter, Doug Bolinger, and the staff at Hunter and Associates, a special thanks for your diligence and grace under pressure.

To my former partners, Jack Canfield and Mark Victor Hansen, Peter Vegso, and the staff of Health Communication Inc. for giving me my introduction to the publishing industry.

To Darlene Patterson, Anna Marie Malfatana, and Kim Marie Fedewa for some of my first introductions at the track.

To Kermit and Miss Lois Marshall and their son, Kenny, for bringing me in to their family.

To Dan and Neva Francis for their continuous prayers, pastoring my family, and faith in me.

The journey of a thousand miles begins with a single step. Last, but not least, I would like to thank Ann and Garland Johnson for finding me funding for my dream, and the entire Doug McClain family, Debra, Autumn, Douglas, Michelle, Chelsea, Paul and John for coming to the aid of my company in its most dire moments.

To all of you, this is your *Healing Voice From the Heart of Racing.*

A very special thanks to the following
contributors to the Petty Family Tradition CD:

- Lee Petty, Richard Petty, Kyle Petty and Adam
  Petty items licensed by Petty Marketing
  Company, LLC.
- Robert Scanlon, Senior V.P. SEEDVISION
- World Sports Enterprises
- Council Bradshaw, Fox 8 Greensboro, NC
- Footage Courtesy International Speedway
  Corporation. Little Circle C ISC. All Rights
  Reserved
- Courtesy of Action Sports Adventure and
  ESPN Enterprises

CONTENTS

CHAPTER ONE   Fast Cars – Kind Hearts . . . 13

EARNHARDT'S THE MAN   *Brian Spivey* 14

PLEASE DON'T QUIT   *Dale Earnhardt, Max Helton and Ron Camacho* .15

I KNOW A MAN   *Dale Earnhardt, Jr.* 19

THE REAL WINNER   *Jeremy Mayfield and Brad Winters* . . 22

ROMANCE GOES FULL CIRCLE   *John Shaughnessy* 24

THE GIFT   *Claire B. Lang* 31

CHAPTER TWO   The Racing Family . . . 35

LOVE AT 20,000 FEET   *Bobby Allison, Max Helton and Ron Camacho* .36

BROTHERS AT THEIR BEST   *Bobby LaBonte and Max Helton* 43

LOOK WHO'S FOLLOWING   *Dale Jarrett, Max Helton and Ron Camacho* 46

WIN ONE FOR ME DADDY   *Darrell Waltrip and Max Helton* 50

JEFF GORDON'S TRAINING WHEELS   *John Bickford and Claire B. Lang* 52

HERMAN THE GERMAN   *Kenny Wallace and Ron Camacho* 54

TELL HER WITH "TATERS"   *Sterling Marlin and Claire B. Lang* . . .62

TAKE CARE OF MY MOTHER   *Eddie Jarvis and Claire B. Lang* . . .63

PASSING ALONG A TRADITION   *Tim Fedewa and Ron Camacho* .65

PREPARING FOR THE ULTIMATE HEALING   *Max Helton* 70

STAYING IN TOUCH   *Kyle Petty and Max Helton* 74

CHAPTER THREE   Racing With Faith . . . 75

AN UNEXPECTED ALLIANCE   *Max Helton* 76

BROKEN TO BECOME BEAUTIFUL   *Susan Santerre* 78

INTIMIDATION INSPIRATION   *Kathy Nelson* 82

FORGIVENESS   *Max Helton* .87

FRONT ROW JOE   *Joe Nemechek and Ron Camacho* 89

THE POWER OF FAMILY   *Brett Bodine* 94

CHAPTER FOUR   The Race . . . 101

BOOING IS GOOD   *Jeff Gordon, Max Helton and Ron Camacho*   .102

TONY STEWART'S THREE WHEELER   *Nelson Stewart and Claire B. Lang*105

"I'M ALIVE!"   *Jimmie Johnson and Claire B. Lang* 106

THE DAY RUSTY WALLACE MADE HISTORY   *Randy J. Poyer* .108

CHOCOLATE   *Chocolate and Caron Meyers* 110

THANKS TO EARNHARDT   *Ernie Irvan and Max Helton* 114

110% AND ON TIME   *Buckshot Jones* 118

A TRUE RACING FAN   *Chris Economacki* 122

MY RACING HAREM   *Bill Venturini and Ron Camacho* 129

MY HEART OF RACING   *Jane Smith* 133

THAT'S RACIN'!   *Tom Mason* 135

CHAPTER FIVE   The Long Road . . . 136

I HAVE DREAMS   *Mark Martin, Max Holton and Ron Camacho* . .137

THE SEASONS IN HIS LIFE   *Kenny Irwin, Sr., B. Winters, R. Camacho* 140

LOST YOUR JOB? HUMPY'S PHONE CALLS   *Claire B. Lang* . .146

GREEN 18   *Jane Smith* 149

TOOTHPICK PHILOSOPHY   *Felix Sabates and Ron Camacho* . . .151

"I GAVE IT ALL I HAD"   *Tony Johns* 153

DECIDING FACTOR   *Greg Davis* 157

MATCHING SCARS   *Bobby Hillin, Jr.* 162

CHAPTER SIX   The Fans . . . 165

HE DID IT HIS WAY   *Karen Fenrich* 166

THE FINISH LINE DECIDES   *Kira Bloomingdale* 169

NASCAR SURE BEATS VACUUM CLEANERS   *Cheryl Walker* .170

CAMP GOOD DAYS   *Jim Rosati* 173

A HERO FOREVER   *Margie Lambert* 175

A CHAMPION'S REWARD   *Ginger Wolfson* 179

AN AMAZING LADY   Susan Tribucher 182

LOVE AND INSPIRATION   DW from SC 184

CHANGE OF HEART   Richard Rabenold 187

KINDNESS IN THE FACE OF ADVERSITY   William Kirk II 190

RUSTY'S BOLT   JAN TEEL 192

I AM A NASCAR FAN   WALTER MABE 194

CHAPTER SEVEN   Memories . . . 196

TREY AND TIA   Barry Dodson, Max Helton and Ron Camacho . 197

DAVEY   Miss Lois, Kermit, and Ron Camacho 202

A HELPING HAND   Stevie Waltrip and Claire B. Lang 206

SOMEONE I NEVER KNEW   Jenni Thompson 208

THE SONG   Claire B. Lang 211

WHAT MAKES A TREASURE   Larry Baldwin 213

CHAPTER EIGHT The Petty Family Tradition . . 215

THE KING   Richard Petty 216

KYLE   Kyle Petty 227

CHAPTER ONE
Fast Cars – Kind Hearts

"I guess Bobby Allison told Neil Bonnett that there was one requirement for membership in the Alabama Gang—to be nice to other people."
Michael Waltrip

Earnhardt's The Man

When my second son, Joshua, was three years old, we read the Bible at night. I was trying to explain the Trinity to him, thinking I was doing a good job. I said "Christ is God, the Son of God who came to live with us for a time. So He is the God and the Man. Joshua spoke up and said, "No, no, Daddy. God is God – Earnhart's the Man!" How can you argue with a three year old?

Brian Spivey

Please Don't Quit

I idolized my dad, Ralph Earnhardt. He was the smartest person I knew. All I ever thought about while I was going to school was hanging out in the shop and working with him. Whatever he was doing seemed far more important to me than studying, whether It was watching him train his bird-hunting dogs, building cars, or taking care of his family. I thought he was it.

When I was sixteen, I wanted to quit school so I could be at the shop and work on cars. I didn't care about any book learning or anything else in life. I didn't think I'd ever need it. My parents were upset when I told them I was quitting. My dad sat me down and had a real long talk with me. He said, "If you finish school, I'll buy you a car." I replied, "Daddy, I don't want to finish school."

So at the first opportunity, I dropped out. I'm sorry now I didn't get the book learning I needed, but my biggest regret is that my father asked me to do something and I didn't do it. You know, you can remember your dad asking you to do chores, but this was something different. He asked me to stay in school because he didn't go to school, and he knew just how important it was for his kids to get a good education and make something of themselves. If I could go back and change the past, I'd finish school for him as much as for myself.

After I left high school, all I wanted to do was work on racecars. I got jobs here and there, but it wasn't until I had married and divorced that I finally figured out how life really is: a storybook deal doesn't happen unless you work for it.

15

After I got the opportunity to drive for Neil Castles in Charlotte, people helped me out so I finally made it in racing. But getting there without being able to spell well, or understand some of the language in contracts and agreements was tough. I could write well, and add well, but to spell words or write a sentence was hard for me. I knew I didn't measure up in book smarts, but I also knew as far as street smarts were concerned, I was pretty well off. You learn what you have to. When I was working on my own racecars and building my own engines, I was doing clearances, and could bore and stroke heads, just like my dad taught me.

It took me a long time to realize that not being educated is nothing to be ashamed of. The worst part of it was not facing it or dealing with it. It's easy to believe that other people are smarter than you and that you're not as good. I sometimes still feel that I'm not as sharp as the next guy when it comes to computers, but I do manage to get the NASCAR monitor up or play a game of solitaire.

Fortunately, in the late '70's, Teresa came along. We hit it off and got married in 1982. It's made my life a whole lot simpler. She's been very positive and supportive, sharing the workload, the responsibility, and the dedication it takes to run a home and a business.

I was always embarrassed about not being able to spell somebody's name correctly or to write a letter or something fairly simple. But after signing thousands of autographs, I've learned that there are many ways to spell Brian and other names.

Since I started winning races and became somewhat famous, I've been working with libraries to promote reading. We did a big poster about reading.

Kannapolis had a big Dale Earnhardt Day. I suggested that they raise money and earmark it for education. They have since bought a lot of computers for the Carrabus County schools and Kannapolis city schools.

When young kids come up and ask me how to become a racecar driver, I tell them to get a good education because racing today is so competitive. Everything helps. If you are a little bit sharper at figuring things out or putting together some formula, it's just another plus, another side of the column you're not short on. It's a big thing for me. I'm not just blowing off steam or passing the buck. I'm very serious when I talk about education. I just don't see how anyone can make it today without an education. When Dale Jr. finished high school, he told me he didn't want to do anything, but he finally agreed to go to Community college. He took computer business and automotive classes. Now he's a computer wiz; he just loves getting online.

Fortunately, I was able to make it without an education. I'd invest the money I won and make it grow. That's where education, street smarts, and Teresa and I work together.

I've been very lucky. I got the right opportunities and breaks. My greatest fear is that kids will look at me and say, "He didn't get an education so I don't need to worry about it." That's the wrong attitude and direction. I want to tell them, "Look how great Dale Earnhardt could have been if he'd had an education. Look how much farther he could have gone. He might own a multi-billion dollar company... he might have been smart enough to become a famous inventor or gotten an earlier step up.

I always tell teenagers, "Please don't quit school." You think, "I can't wait to start my life; I've got to get into racing." But in order to go forward, you first need to finish what you started. That's very important in life. For me, not completing my education is unfinished business. There is always a part of me that feels incomplete and I still harbor the grief of not doing something my father asked me to do.

Dale Earnhardt, Max Helton and Ron Camacho

I Know A Man

I just sit down in front of the computer and spill it out. It doesn't take but about 15 or 20 minutes to do if you're in the middle of some heavy thinking. I've read a lot. I read a lot of articles about myself and that's where I learned the most about writing and how to express myself in the written word. Basically, when I'm sitting down in front of that computer to write, I'm just telling a story or something's bothering me. I try to be honest without ticking anybody off or without upsetting my father or my family or embarrassing myself or regretting anything.

I probably wrote six or seven columns, but the only ones that have been out are the ones that have been approved. The other ones are either too personal or the person I'm writing them about wouldn't like it, so I don't let anybody see it. It's just a way for me to express how I'm feeling:

"I Know a Man"

I know a man whose hands are so callused that gloves aren't necessary. Once, while cutting down a tree, he cut the back of his hand to the bone with a chainsaw. He didn't even stop to look until the job was done.

I've seen him get thrown from a tractor. The tractor, as large as a small home, was flipped by the trunk of a stubborn oak tree. His first thought was not fear, but how quickly he could get the tractor back on its tracks to complete the task. He has suffered broken bones and never had one complaint. Not to anyone, not even to himself.

This man could lead the world's finest army. He has wisdom that knows no bounds. No fire could burn his character, no stone could break it. He maintains a private existence, one that shelters his most coveted thoughts from the world.

His upbringing was no controlled creation. His hard-working family was like many from that era. He gained his knowledge in hard dirt and second-hand tools, from his toys as a child to the trucks he drove in his 20's. From that natural upbringing, he has an incredible sense of good and bad. He sees it before it sees him, in people, in anything imaginable. Where did he learn this? How does he know so many things?

I've seen this man create many things. With no blueprints, he has carved and produced wonders upon wonders. His resume shows he has created major companies. He has hammered out deal upon deal – always being as fair as God would have it. He has taken land with thick shrubs and deep valleys and molded them into a frontier fit for heaven. He has built homes that kings couldn't fathom.

Solving problems is as easy as breathing for him. They are thrown his way like the morning paper. People surround him daily, wanting solutions. He hands them out with pride and passion. Each solution is a battle won. He calculates his every action, demanding the same from everyone else. He is honest in letting you know your end of the bargain.

His friendship is the greatest gift you could ever obtain. Out of all his attributes, it is the most impressive. He trusts only a few with this gift. If you ever break that trust – it is over. He accepts few apologies. Many have crossed him and they leave with only regret for their actions. In every result, he stands as an example of what hard work and dedication will achieve. Even his enemies know this.

I have had the pleasure of joining him on the battlefield. I have experienced his intimidating wrath. That may sound strong, but I know what I am talking about. He roams like a lion, king of his jungle. His jungle is his and his alone. Every step he takes has purpose. Every walk has reason.

He praises God, loves his family, and enjoys his friends.

I wonder what his future holds. He has so much to be proud of. To this point, he's only barely satisfied. His eyes see much more than my imagination could produce. He is Dale Earnhardt. Dad, the world's finest army awaits.

Dale Earnhardt, Jr.

"To me, the real heroes are the people who do worthwhile things without the thought of monetary gain." Benny Parsons

The Real Winner

Six year-old Cassie Boone was in a struggle for survival. Already a victim of cerebral palsy, life had suddenly become tougher. She rested in her hospital bed at Riley Children's Hospital in Indianapolis, Indiana with her stomach laid open and exposed from surgery. Family and hospital staff would come to her side, but most visitors found the sight too unbearable. Even the family priest would stand in the doorway for prayer and apologize as he quickly exited into the hallway.

One day a visitor entered the room. He walked next to Cassie's bed, gently took her hand, stroked her hair, and sat down by her side. His name was Jeremy Mayfield, a fresh young face on the NASCAR Winston Cup racing circuit. In town for the 1995 Brickyard 400 race, Jeremy had come to Riley Children's Hospital unannounced, and without any media, to visit the children. He asked Cassie about her family, her friends, her hobbies, and her illness. Cassie was overjoyed with the attention she received from her new friend. Her smile was one that her family will always remember. Jeremy stocked Cassie up with hats and other gifts he had brought along. When he sensed Cassie growing tired he squeezed her hand, said goodbye, and left to visit another child. On that day, Jeremy Mayfield became a hero to the Boone family.

Eighteen months after Jeremy's visit, Cassie unexpectedly lost her battle for life. Although each day is difficult, her family has found comfort knowing that, for the first time, Cassie has a perfect body in heaven. They also find comfort in the fond memories Cassie has left behind. One of those memories is the visit Jeremy made with Cassie. "'I will never forget the joy on Cassie's face that day," said Cassie's mother, Linda. "Her smile seemed to last forever. Jeremy will always be special to our family."

Jeremy Mayfield had a breakout year in 1998. The Owensboro, Kentucky native became one of the Winston Cup point leaders, finishing in seventh place for the year and winning his first Winston Cup race. He was suddenly on the cover of every NASCAR magazine. Everyone loves a winner and, on the track, Jeremy had become a winner. But to the Boone family, and to the other children at Riley Hospital on a hot summer day in 1995, Jeremy Mayfield showed that he was already a winner. To touch the heart of a child, to bring a smile through the pain, to bring a ray of hope in a life of defeat, to give a family a memory that will always bring joy... that is a victory that matters.

Jeremy Mayfield and Brad Winters

Romance Goes Full Circle

Stooped and gray-haired, the man used his burned stump of a left hand to help him push the wheelchair of his seemingly catatonic wife around the roller rink's glossy wooden floor. He smiled, swaying the chair to the music, as if they alone were dancing under the swirling stars cascading down from the rotating mirrored ball on the ceiling.

None of the other skaters recognized the man, although he is one of the most successful drivers in the history of racing, a former Indianapolis 500 racer and a ten-time national champion who still competes at age 66. Nor did they know that the lifeless woman was once an accomplished painter and sculptor. Sadly, none of them knew they were witnessing one of the last hauntingly beautiful chapters of a great love story born more than 35 years ago at this same Illinois skating rink.

"She smelled good," Mel Kenyon confided, smiling as he recalled the first time he met his future wife. She was blond, blue-eyed, a decade younger than he and at five-feet nine-inches, taller by an inch. He knew instantly she was something special.

At 30, in 1963, Mel was a man who enjoyed gliding around roller-skating rinks almost as much as he loved roaring around racetracks. On that fateful day, he laced up his skates and took to the floor just as a "bell skate" was announced. That meant males and females on the floor suddenly became pairs and skated in tandem. Every time the manager rang a bell, each man would separate from his partner and join hands with the girl ahead of him.

24

That's how Mel met Marieanne. He wasn't too keen on it, but he had to let her skate with the other guys as the bell skate continued. However, when the music stopped, he sped to her side. For the rest of the evening, they foxtrotted, two-stepped, and waltzed together on skates. A week later, he asked her to a movie. Smitten, and by this time convinced she was "the one," he put her to his ultimate test. He invited her to one of his races. She enjoyed it, which clinched the deal. Six months later, he proposed; a year later, they were newlyweds.

Then came the incident Mel refers to as "the bonfire," a racing accident that nearly killed him and forever changed his life and his relationship with Marieanne.

In June, 1965, on the 27th lap at the Langhorne Race Track, Mel's car blew an engine, spun around, and bounced off the wall, rendering him unconscious before coming to a full stop. But before anyone had a chance to react, two other cars slammed into the car from behind. The explosion turned Mel's car into an inferno. Flames engulfed the vehicle, which then torpedoed across the infield of the Pennsylvania track. Only quick-thinking action by national champion Joe Leonard, saved his life. He and two others managed to drag him from the four-wheel incinerator, but not before the fire ravaged his body. "I was in the fire for three minutes before a jeep got there with fire bottles," Mel says, still shuddering at the memory. Forty percent of his body--including face, chest, and legs--was covered by third-degree burns. His left hand was burned to a stump.

"Marieanne got one of those phone calls a wife never wants to get," he says. "We had been married only a year and two months. When she saw me, she didn't recognize me. I was all wrapped up [in bandages] from head to foot, like a mummy. [Doctors] had to put my nose back on and rearrange my face. There were seventeen operations. We didn't have any kids yet, so I was her first baby. For a month she fed me and did everything for me."

Marieanne also helped him change his life in a positive way. "She had been working on me all the time to find the Lord, but until [I was in] the burn center, it didn't happen," he admits. "With Marieanne's help, I turned over what was left of my miserable life to the Lord Jesus, [asking Him] to do with me what He wanted, not what I wanted."

"Twelve doctors said I'd be in the burn center for nine months or better," he continues. "With the Lord's help and healing, I was ready to leave two weeks after I gave my life to Him. In all, it was three months...not nine."

The accident not only brought Mel closer to God, it also brought him and Marieanne even closer as a couple.

Mel returned to racing in February 1966, using prosthesis on his left hand to help him steer. With Marieanne cheering him on, he began a comeback that would lead him to his first appearance in the Indianapolis 500 that same year. Marieanne admired the way Mel approached each race with a desire to push to the limit himself and his car. He, in turn, loved her artistic ability and the way she was willing to tackle anything, including teaching disabled children how to swim.

Marieanne's dedication to racing went above and beyond the call of duty. "When I was injured in 1969 in

Michigan, she fashioned up a crutch for me," he smiles, adding, "then I directed her to take apart the bent race car so we could fix it. She was pregnant with Vaughn at the time."

By the time Vaughn and his younger brother, Brice, were born, Mel's driving career centered on racing midget cars. During the summer, the family of four followed the midget racing tour through the United States; when the weather turned cold, they headed down under, to compete in New Zealand and Australia. There was plenty to smile and celebrate through those years as Mel continued to rack up the victories--379 total now--and national championships.

Vaughn Kenyon recalls his father being "almost unbeatable." And his mother, he says, "… used to do the portraits of the Indianapolis 500 winners; she was right there with every aspect of our childhood...it was all a lot of fun. We did almost everything together as a family."

In 1991, the day before Mel was to compete in the first annual Mel Kenyon Classic--a race established in his honor at the Indianapolis Raceway Park--the family ran headfirst into another of life's speed bumps. This time, it was Marieanne's turn. An avid bicyclist, Marieanne each morning routinely rode 15 to 20 miles before going to work at an electronic assembly company in Lebanon, Indiana. On that particular morning in late August, Mel realized she was late getting home, but didn't make any connection when an ambulance sped by their house, sirens wailing.

"It happened about a mile from our house," Mel remembers. "An airline flight controller who lives nearby saw it all. She was coming home when a neighbor's dog ran right at her bike. Evidently, she put the brakes on, but couldn't stop. When the wheel turned, the bike dumped her and slammed her head against the pavement." Marieanne's body rolled over, but her head--still topped with a helmet--stayed, twisting her spinal cord and neck." She was Life-Flighted to a hospital, and Mel rushed there to see her.

The doctors' faces were grim as they explained Marieanne's serious injuries. She'd hurt the right side of her head, the same spot she'd injured in a bike accident three years before. While she lay still and unresponsive in her hospital bed, Mel stayed by her side, touching her, recalling the ten times he'd been knocked unconscious while racing; the ten times he'd always recovered mentally. He fervently prayed that God would now spare his wife, too.

But it wasn't to be. Marieanne remained unresponsive. "She couldn't walk, talk, or move," he says, slowly shaking his head. "After six months, I had an MRI done on her. They said there was no hope of recovery."

Despite the demanding health care Marieanne now required, Mel refused to put her in a nursing home. He knew he could never walk away from her. The memory of Marieanne's unfailing devotion to him during those excruciating months he spent in the burn center was still deeply etched in his soul. He instead brought her home, propped her up in a wheelchair and pushed her through the house, stopping in her art-filled studio where she'd spent endless hours painting and sculpting. He also took her along to his national and international speaking engagements. He gave inspirational talks about "The Sudden Stop in Life," of finding God, and not losing hope when tragedy strikes.

"You never know when the sudden stops will

happen," he says, "but they will happen...like my bonfire, like Marieanne's bike accident," he says. "So having the Lord on your side prior to the sudden stops makes it a whole lot easier to accept, adjust to, and overcome."

When people saw Mel "dancing" with Marieanne at the roller rink or at his lectures, most saw a woman who seemed to be completely unresponsive to life. But Mel knew differently. He noticed how she could move her left leg and her left foot in time to music. He saw how she followed a conversation, and talked with her eyes--one blink for "no," and several for "yes." And he knew the trips to the roller rink were just as good for her as they were for him.

In December, 1999, Mel began making arrangements to bring Marieanne to her parents' home in Illinois, where they traditionally celebrated Christmas. He also looked forward to taking her for their annual spin around the roller rink where they'd met so long ago. Two days before their December 16 departure, Mel awoke next to his wife, completely unaware that yet another sudden--and final--stop loomed immediately ahead. "I cleaned her up, then I got back into bed with her," he says, closing his eyes, trying to keep the tears inside as he remembers the morning she died. "We held hands; I told her how good she was doing and wished her the Lord's blessing. Then we went back to sleep. I woke up to feed her at 8:30, but she was already gone."

Today, tears flow easily as he recalls how she died by his side, how he bathed his 56-year-old wife, washed her hair, and dressed her before taking her body to the funeral home. He brushes them away, explaining that during the past eight years and four months, he never once felt burdened by taking care of Marieanne. "The Lord loves us, and we're to love our mate through thickness and thin," he says simply. "It was a pleasure doing it for her because she had done it for me. It was just love."

John Shaughnessy

The Gift

It was the week before Christmas at WSOC FM 103.7, Charlotte, North Carolina's country music giant. This heritage flagship station has broadcast the heartbeat of racers and their sport in the home of stock car racing for as long as most folks can remember.

Nothing feels as lonely as a radio studio during the early morning shift at holiday time. But on this cold, December morning, the female half of the morning team felt more alone than ever. Her co-host had already departed for the holidays and it seemed to her that the listeners were away as well. In fact, the only life in the vast, deserted studio seemed to be the memories of broadcasts from years past.

There was the day Kelley Earnhardt called the show from Dallas, Texas to broadcast a birthday wish to her famous father, Dale. Darrell Waltrip was listening that day and called to ask why the station was broadcasting Earnhardt birthday wishes but nothing for the birthday of his brother Michael.

That's when the Earnhardts and the Waltrips began an impromptu radio feud to see which family could have the most members call in birthday greetings. Michael Waltrip's wife, Buffy, called, then a sister from Kentucky, another brother and, finally, even Mama Waltrip. Earnhardt's two other grown children, his sister, and even his mother called. The entire living family trees of Earnhardts and Waltrips burned up the station hot-lines, making competitive on-air birthday phone call wishes. Darrell Waltrip called back, disguising his voice as his father's to break a tie. The

31

hosts recognized his prank and the call was ruled ineligible. Just as the show signed off, the real Leroy Waltrip called in and the contest was over. Mr. Waltrip is gone now, but his phone call to beat the Earnhardts is a treasured memory that will never leave the studio.

There was the time a young, skinny boy named Dale Earnhardt, Jr. agreed to go on the air to fill a slot during race week when Earnhardt himself was not available. "Why put him on?" Someone asked. "Couldn't you get the real Earnhardt?" But the boy had already been booked on the show. He was so quiet he barely spoke and so skinny he was hardly even visible. After he said a soft hello on-air, he quietly walked over to a racing simulator nearby and beat nearly every big-name Winston Cup driver in attendance who would take him on. That skinny boy who some questioned as a legitimate guest is also gone and, in his place, is a brilliant superstar who graces billboards and national television spots and who earns a fortune. They fight and push to get their microphone to him now. Inside, he has not changed.

Jeff Gordon was a regular on-air guest. He told the listeners how embarrassed he was when he ran out of gas in his personal car on busy streets in Charlotte, North Carolina twice while dating Brooke, who became his wife. His message on air was always down-to-earth and of constant faith. He admitted that being booed by fans was, at first, painful. Winning was almost impossible to avoid then. He was a young boy who could not lose. That boy is also only a memory now, replaced by a very rich man, who, in his success, never lost his strength of character or his faith.

She thought, with a smile, about Dale Earnhardt's favorite song, by Alabama, "...I'm in a hurry to get things done, I rush and rush until life's no fun. All you really have to do is live and die and I'm in a hurry and don't know why..." The station played it regularly for him around race time. Dale Earnhardt could have any song in the music library played for him, and yet the man who races for a living on the track picks a song that reminds him to slow down off of it.

The rise of the morning light shifted thoughts from memories to reality. On this particular broadcast day, the racers were long gone on off-season holiday vacations. The host was assigned to work that day because of the Forgotten Angels, a project to solicit Christmas toys for poor children. She was there to communicate the fact that the station Christmas tree still had ornaments listing the names of Forgotten Angels--children with no gifts--and the holiday was a mere breath away.

The host felt a momentary sense of gloom. Christmas song after Christmas song seemed to ride airwaves that reached a town already gone elsewhere. Her efforts to communicate the plight of the children seemed to be resonating into a void until the mood was broken by the flickering red light of the studio hot line. The caller was a male voice asking if there were still angels on the tree unclaimed. "Yes," she answered, putting little validity into the call.

"Well," the man said, "there is someone listening who would like to help. Within an hour, a man with a check will arrive at the station. Take that check and buy presents for all the children on the tree who have not been claimed. One condition though, the donor would like to remain anonymous."

As her shift ended and she prepared to leave the isolated building, she thought very little about the predawn call. Passing the lobby where the station Christmas tree stood, she noticed the Forgotten Angel ornaments hanging from its branches. The unclaimed children's names beckoned a lonely call. As she hurried out the door to her car, she nearly passed the man who called out her name. "Yes," she replied, walking over to him. The man handed her an envelope and left.

To her surprise, the envelope contained a large check made out to the Forgotten Angels. It took her a moment to comprehend the generous gift before she noticed the signature on the check. The moment of realization is meaningful even to this day. As was agreed, he never got on-air credit for his good deed and his name was never announced. But, at a time when the call went out for help and it seemed that no one heard it, there was someone listening. He was a man well known for his generosity—team owner, Rick Hendrick.

This story is true. I know it to be so because I was there. I'm Claire B. Lang and I was the announcer.

Claire B. Lang

CHAPTER TWO
The Racing Family

"The good Lord directs some of us, and I consider it a privilege to have found what I really wanted to do at an early age."
H. A. "Humpy" Wheeler

Love at 20,000 Feet

Flying was the one place where I felt I could be myself. Up in the clouds, away from everyone, I was still Bobby Allison...still at the controls...still a man people looked up to. Twenty thousand feet up, it's almost as if the 1988 crash at Pocono International Raceway never happened. As long as I stayed in the air, I could forget I ever suffered the head injury that ended my racing career.

After that accident, I had a tremendous loss of self-confidence. I couldn't remember things, my emotions were out-of-control, and I was no longer able to address the business of business. See, I was never good at business before my injury. I was the best racer, but I was also one of the worst businessmen in the whole industry. I was always going to solve the problem by winning the race and paying the bills. That philosophy worked all the way through the 1988 Daytona 500. Through my career, I've paid for rides and made all kinds of concessions, then gone and won the race. And I never took the attitude that you guys wouldn't have won this race without me and the car.... never did. So here I'm struggling with all of this stuff. I had a race team with my name on it and also had a lot of influence because I owned Bobby Allison Motorsports. But after I was injured, some of my management people weren't conducting business the way they should have, so I had sponsors telling me, "Bobby, you need to straighten it up." People were saying, "Boy, your race team isn't doing good enough." All I could do was smile and nod my head. I had people who worked for me that would say, "Go in your office, sit down, and shut up." I would go in my office and shut up. If someone yelled at me, I sat down and cried. I couldn't stand it. And I couldn't stand for Judy to be mad at me.

My confidence problem left me always looking for a compliment; it didn't matter where I was. Compliments help people carry on no matter what the situation is. They help them through the tough times; they help them enjoy the good times. If the situation is bad, a compliment makes you feel better. When I first started racing, my good friend, Ray Armstrong, told me, "Listen, kid, every request for an autograph is a compliment." It still is. But after I was injured, I couldn't race anymore so I wasn't getting as many compliments. But when I climbed in the airplane, I could get away from all that. Flying was the one thing I could still do without involving the people from the shop in Charlotte. And I was really confident that the one paid employee that I had was tremendously on my side. But after I was injured, I lost him and didn't even know it. He found out that if he wanted his way all he had to do was yell at me. In fact, the day Judy fired him, he took my $30,000 prop balancer and was walking to his truck with it. I said, "That's mine," and he shouted, "You gave it to me!" So I said, "Okay, okay...take it!" and he walked off with my $30,000 prop balancer. I was still struggling with all of this when Clifford was killed in a Busch Grand Nationals practice run at the Michigan Speedway on August 13, 1992. Then the following July, my oldest boy, Davey, died of injuries he suffered when his helicopter crashed at Talladega. The irony of that whole thing is that Clifford played, played, played and got killed working, and Davey worked, worked, worked and got killed playing.

In my early recovery, Clifford would say, "Come on, Dad, go with me...Come on, Dad, tell me what to do on this car." It really, really helped me a lot. I was enjoying Clifford's effort, and then that tragedy happened. It was tough...really, really tough.

Early on, Judy and I didn't support each other in the healing process. I went in one direction and she went in another. We just didn't seem to be anywhere on the same page in our daily lives. A big part of my problem was my head injury. I was really tangled up in my thinking. I really struggled, but people thought I was doing fine. I smiled and nodded my head, and they would say, "Oh man, that guy's fixed!" And you know, I would be so out of touch with what was going on that when I think of it now, it amazes me. I was so bitter. I was mad at God...bitter and mad at anything and everything. I don't know if there was anything we could have done to prevent the divorce. There was one trauma on top of a trauma. I was really pretty convinced I was right in my attitude and I was really mad at her. I felt like she had disagreed with me at a time when I really wanted her to agree with me. I was all tangled up in my thinking and divorce seemed inevitable.

When Judy moved out, I quite honestly thought she had a boyfriend. When I would be in North Carolina, she would be in Alabama; then I would go to Alabama and she would go to North Carolina. I didn't know that when she took the apartment for two years, she was thinking and hoping that we would gradually come back together. I was really unhappy with us and I was really unhappy with Davey's widow, Liz, too. Liz decides she's going to get married and it's a guy that seems to be neat from a neat family. It seems to be a really positive thing. But I was not going to go to the wedding. My daughter says, "Dad, you have to go to the wedding...you have to go." So I drove to Spartanburg for the David Pearson celebration on Friday. I had wrecked the airplane so I had to drive. I got a motel room there and planned to drive through, the day Saturday to get to Nashville for the wedding that evening. In Spartanburg, we got the message that Adam Petty was killed. It really had a strange effect on me. I felt really hurt about it, but was once again confused. I felt sorry for Richard, Linda, Kyle and Patti but I didn't want to go to North Carolina. A little of it was my own mental deficit and a little was the agony of Clifford and Davey. So when I drove to Nashville the next day and I decided I was going to think about stuff that makes me feel good...about airplanes, people I'm dating, that I'm going to that wedding and even if I'm annoyed with Liz, at least she's marrying a guy that ain't the guy that annoys me the worst. So I got to Nashville. The wedding was in this big church. There were lots of people and I'm on the aisle in about the twentieth row. My mom is next to me and my niece, Michelle, is next to her. The first thing that happens is that Liz is coming up the aisle and she stops and says, "Hello, Grandma. Thanks for coming." I said, "That was really neat! Here's a girl going up to get married and she stops and says something special to my 93-year-old mother."

Then I saw Judy up there with Liz's family. She looked pretty nice. When the wedding was over, she met me at the door of the church and said, "We should put aside our differences and go help the Pettys." And I said, 'Yes, we should." So that immediately changed the situation. I spent time with her at the wedding reception Saturday night. The next morning, she picked me up at my hotel so we could drive to North Carolina. The first hour on the road, it was friendly. I drove and it was a chance for me to say a lot of things I wanted to say whether she liked it or not. For the first time, I talked and she listened. Then she talked and I listened. As we drove on up the road, we agreed that we had made a lot of mistakes along the way, but the really horrible mistake was to get a divorce. I have to be honest...my original motivation in this whole deal was to get a discount on alimony. I thought the alimony I was paying---$6000 a month---was ridiculous. But when I saw Judy there at the wedding, I finally had to admit to myself, "That is still the girl I'm in love with." On the one hand, I wanted to hurt her, but on the other hand, I wanted to protect her from anything and everything. We had four children and they are the neatest children any family could ever have...and credit certainly has to go to her for producing them and raising them from little babies. The greatest compliment a parent can have is that their child is loved around the world. And Davey still is.

When we headed back to Alabama, I was still trying to sort through everything that was going on. I had to say that I was truly still not playing with a full deck, but I knew it was a hand I had to play. So I told her, "Maybe we should remarry and do our best to put everything in the past behind us and go forward. Once a priest told us in the eyes of the Catholic Church we were still married, we went to the courthouse in Bessemer on Richard Petty's birthday. He found out a week later that we got married on July 3rd at 12:12...and his old racecar number was three twelve. As to putting the past behind us...that's easier said than done, but I think we've done a pretty good job of that. We communicate better now. And we're in a really unusual situation...for the first time in our lives, we have time to spend with each other. In Hueytown, we had the children, my mother and my dad, and then we had a daily parade of race fans. After Clifford and Davey were killed, one of the really toughest things for us was that I wanted to stay in Hueytown and she wanted to get away from it. I mistakenly related that to her interest in someone else rather than her unhappiness with the constant tourists. People would drive up in front of the house and get out of their car, crying and carrying on and saying, "Oh, I love Davey." You know, it's so incredibly gripping when someone does that, but then the second person does it. On some days, we'd have three or four groups of people come by. When they'd leave, Judy would be a basket case.

For most of our married life, I was busy doing the work that I thought was important to do and felt she should pay attention to it, and she was taking care of the kids and doing domestic stuff around the house and wanted me to pay attention to that. So there was a lack of communication both ways. Then she would try to tell me something and I wouldn't listen. And I would tell her something and she wouldn't listen. In the midst of all of this, I have a friend who tells me, "Aw, don't worry about that." And her friend's telling her the same thing. Well, every married couple should worry about that—both sides, husband and wife! I was a mess all the way up to the end. For the longest time, I could not tell Judy that I loved her. I mean, I knew right from the beginning, but I couldn't tell her that. She had to pull it out of me. It took about three or four weeks before I could just say it. Later I found out that Judy was going through the same thing. But now, we both know that this is love, and not just a desire to get the house or money back.

Bobby Allison, Max Helton and Ron Camacho

Brothers at Their Best

Our family is modest, so we don't talk about things like this much, but I'll never forget that day in Atlanta. When it was over, Terry and I just said, "Man, I just can't believe that happened." It was a great day for all of our family--our wives, our mom and dad were all there.

My brother, Terry, and I were not close friends while I was growing up. There were eight years between us, so we had different friends. Both of us were born in Corpus Christi, Texas. Terry grew up mostly in Texas and was off racing all over the state. While my growing up years were more in North Carolina, having moved there with my family when I was still in school. Now that Terry and I live near each other and are racing in the same series, we have gotten much closer and are good friends.

It just happened in November of 1996 that we went to Atlanta for the last race of the year. We couldn't have planned it any better if we'd wanted to. Terry was leading in points for the Winston Cup championship and it had been about 12 years since his last and only championship, so I knew that it would mean so much to him to win this championship. Terry needed a good finish to win. If Jeff Gordon (second in points) won the race, Terry would have to finish eighth or ninth. Terry was looking for his second championship. I was looking for my first win of the season. I had won three races in the last year, but none this year. So both of us were on a mission.

We went out to qualify and I won the pole and Terry started third. Jeff Gordon was second. Terry had struggled with a broken hand since the last race at

Phoenix. He didn't get to practice much and wasn't feeling well. The night before the race, Terry said to me, "Man, I sure do need to lead a lap tomorrow." I assured him that I would do all that I could to help him do that. We also did something very unusual for us to do before a race. We talked about how neat it would be for me to win the race and him to win the championship.

The next morning as I was walking to my car, the Atlanta track public relations guy told me to be sure to come to Victory Lane if Terry won the championship. I commented that I was hoping to be there already. I could not believe that I was saying this, but I did feel good about the race.

I jumped out front at the green flag and led the race. Jeff had some tire problems and had to pit. Terry drove up to me and I let him pass me so that he could collect five bonus points for leading a lap. We both ran well all day. All during the race, I kept up with Terry's position on the track. Never for a moment did I lose sight of where he was and where he needed to be to win the championship. Near the end of the race, Terry dropped back after a pit stop. I knew that he needed to finish in the top five or better to be safe, but Gordon had worked his way back to the front and was still running well, too. I was focused on what I had to do, but it was kind of neat to know what was going on with Terry. The checkered flag waved in the air as I crossed the finish line first. I had won my first race of the season. Gordon finished third. Terry won the championship with a fifth place finish.

Then it happened! Terry and I hadn't discussed anything about what we would do in this situation. After a win, I usually head down pit road to Victory Circle. I just never do unusual things like victory laps or "cutting donuts" on the front stretch. As I was about to turn off the racetrack onto pit road, I noticed Terry drive by on the way to meet the Winston people (series sponsors) on the backstretch, who then would escort him to the front stretch for his celebration. At the last second, I swerved back onto the track to join Terry. We suddenly found ourselves side by side riding around the track together. (That made lots of headlines.) It was awfully exciting! I looked over at Terry and gave him "thumbs up." The fans were going crazy, screaming at us with excitement. My thoughts turned to the uniqueness of this event. One that is so rare in racing that it had never happened before in NASCAR and probably will not happen again for many years to come.

As I drove along side Terry, I started thinking about what we had talked about the night before. I just couldn't believe we had said something that actually became reality. My excitement was more for my parents. How neat it was for them. I pictured them walking proudly to the victory celebrations for their two sons. I thought of my mom and dad having two children and both of them won today in the same race. That is something I'll cherish forever. I won the race and Terry won the championship.

Bobby LaBonte and Max Helton

Look Who's Following

My mom and dad brought up my brother, sister, and me with faith. My dad, Ned Jarrett--also a NASCAR champion--was racing 60 to 70 times a year, so we were on the road a lot. When we were home, we attended church as much as possible; when we were on the road, the Christian values instilled in us didn't change.

My dad is a very driven person. He wanted to succeed and be the best at whatever he was doing, whether it was in the racecar, or being the best promoter at the racetrack after he retired. He had the best short track going at the time, and when he got into broadcasting, he worked hard to be the best...but he didn't do it in a way that he was stepping over people.

He had everyone's best interest at heart, whether it was his family or someone in the business. He's a good example of showing that you can be very successful without being ruthless, as we see in many cases now.

At the time my dad was driving, there were a lot of shady dealings going on at the track. But Dad believed if he worked harder and used the powers that he had, it would benefit him more. He has always had a very strong faith in the Lord and felt it would carry him a lot farther than the other things that were going on at that time.

I do a lot of listening and praying to God, too. I have certainly been blessed in many, many ways--not only on the racetrack, but also with my entire family.

In '95, I was in the Texaco car for Robert Yates.

That was a one-year deal and I knew it was going to be up; Ernie Irvan was going to be back to drive the car the next year. My reason for going to Robert's in the first place, leaving a great situation that I had at Joe Gibbs' operation, was for the opportunity to own my own team. I had owned my own Busch team for a number of years and I felt I could have a successful Winston Cup team if I could find a sponsorship. Robert had agreed to help me, but it didn't work out.

Another opportunity from Robert Yates came along just as we were in final negotiations with a sponsorship proposal from Hooters Restaurants. I could have my own team. We were in the process of putting everything together and had just met with the people from Hooters. The money they offered was a little shy of what I needed, but they had assured me they would help me attain an associate sponsorship. Robert Yates had agreed to do the engines for me, so we were pretty much on our way.

As my wife and I discussed it, we decided that it just wasn't the best situation for me, as far as the image we tried to project. There is nothing wrong with the food at Hooters or it's atmosphere. It wasn't something that I felt completely comfortable with. I began to think that trying to raise a family while having to make thirty appearances at Hooters might not be the best situation. By making promotional appearances at that kind of place, I think it would be difficult for the majority of Christians out there to take my testimony seriously.

So we prayed for something else to come along and it did. Before I signed that contract with Hooters on the Wednesday before Bristol, Robert Yates came to me and asked if I would be interested in driving a

Ford-sponsored car for the second team he was starting. Things do work in a hurry if you talk to the Lord about them! After a lot of soul-searching and praying, the answer was there. It was easy for me to make the choice. Up until that time the best I had finished was fourth in the points.

I was happy with what was going on, but certainly in making that decision--the right decision. It was the best thing for my family. Since then, we've won a championship and a lot of races. It proves that if you listen and follow what God has to tell you, you are going to be rewarded.

I remembered a story my dad once told me about how our actions can affect others. One day he was racing on a dirt track and quickly realized during practice that once the race started, if he was going to be successful, he would have to pick certain objects above the dust to serve as markers. Then, when he saw the markers, he'd know it was time to turn.

Sure enough, soon after the race started, the dust built up quickly. He couldn't even see the car in front of him, but Dad was prepared. He began looking for his markers and it worked. Lap after lap, he navigated the track, using the markers as his guide.

All was going well until he was driving hard down the backstretch into turn three. He couldn't see his marker, but he knew something was coming up soon. All of a sudden, the track got real bumpy. It was obvious something wasn't right. Once the dust cleared, he realized the car he was using as a marker in turn three was gone and he was in the parking lot!

It was quite a sight, but what made it even more interesting was that a group of other racecars were right behind him! Now, Dad realized why he was sitting in the parking lot, but he got out to ask other drivers why they were there. They simply said, "You're the champion. We couldn't see anything either, so we've been following you!"

Dale Jarrett, Max Helton and Ron Camacho

Win One For Me Daddy

The 1987 season was a tough year. Up to that point, I was at the top of the world of racing. I had won three Winston Cup championships. I had won about 70 races in Winston Cup and many poles. Racing had been very good to me. But in 1987, I was with a new team and things weren't going very well. It had been expected that this new team would go gangbusters. We were the dream team. I had the best of backing from the Hendrick Motorsports group, an excellent sponsorship, and the best engine builder in racing. However, going into the last part of the season, we still had not won a race. This had not happened to me since I got my first NASCAR Winston Cup win in 1975.

In addition to my not winning races, we found out that Stevie, my wife, was pregnant. All of this was emotionally tough for me. Stevie had three miscarriages previously, including one in 1986. She had never been able to carry a baby to full term and this was upsetting to me. I leaned on her so much. She is my best friend and had always been with me at every race.

Now she was not able to go to the track each weekend with me. That was difficult. Stevie has always been such a part of my life and my racing career. We had always gone to races together. I had not experienced life at the track without Stevie. I have been deeply in love with her since we met in high school back in Owensboro, Kentucky. She has stood by me with much encouragement through the ups and downs, and boos and cheers of fans. She had set a new standard in racing by being a part of my race team on Sundays at a time when woman were not allowed in the pits. It was tough on me to be racing without her there.

On September 17, we were blessed with our first child, Jessica Leigh. We were very excited! I had to leave to go on to the next race later that week. The race was at Martinsville, Virginia, where I had won several times before. But I had no expectations of winning this time.

As the race progressed I really had no hope of winning, as I was a lap down with just 25 laps to go. Dale Earnhardt was leading. When he stopped for fuel I got back on the lead lap. Then a caution came out with about seven laps to go. On the restart, I was in third place behind Earnhardt and Terry LaBonte. Both of these guys were previous champions and were tough, hard racers. There was no way that I was going to get by them with just a few laps to go. They could make it very difficult to get around them. On the final lap in the final turns of three and four, Terry had gotten up beside Dale and left just a little opening for me to pass both of them, beating them to the finish line. I won my first race of the year!

It was much more special, though, than just being my first win of the season and my first victory with the new team. For earlier that Sunday morning, appearing from nowhere, I was surprised to find a little rosebud in the seat of my car with a note that said, "Win one for me, Daddy!" My first race of the season was sweetened by it occurring on the same day that I was first called "Daddy."

Darrell Waltrip and Max Helton

Jeff Gordon's Training Wheels

Jeff's first bicycle was terrible. I'm almost embarrassed to tell you about it...eight inch wheels with hard rubber tires—not cool at all! All the kids were older and he was just dying to ride his bike with all of them. There was a BMX track at the top of the street, controlled by the Police Athletic League. Jeff had training wheels on his bike. I took them off and told Jeff, "I've got to go to the office. I'll be back in a couple of hours. You need to learn to ride this bike or I'm going to have to put it in the back of the truck and take it to the dump because I'm embarrassed to have it around the house. If you're not going to ride it, we'll get rid of it." (His mother and I had this all planned out.)

We lived on a street with a little hill. I had tried to help Jeff a little bit with learning to ride, but he wasn't quite there yet. He was panic-stricken as I was leaving because he was going to lose his bike and all the other kids had a bike and he wouldn't have one. His mom told him, "Just learn to ride the bike. You've got two hours."

After about an hour, I called home to ask how he was doing. His mom told me he was doing terrible. I said, "Okay, I'll stay out a little longer." After about two hours, I called again and his mom told me she thought it was time for me to come on home.

I came around the corner toward the house and, sure enough, there was Jeff. He pushed off the curb and, because he was going so fast down the hill, I don't think he *could* fall off. He was actually peddling his bike and riding. That's how he got started with riding.

He was so small that we had to make him a bike from scratch for his fifth birthday. I took a frame and modified it. We used wheel chair spokes because they were the lightest spokes I could find. We made magnesium forks and modified 10-speed aluminum cranks. We had the coolest bike on the block; the only one of It's kInd. The only thIng left to do was go race it. After his mom saw a few kids much bigger than Jeff crash on bicycles, she said, "We need to find a new sport." I brought home two quarter-midget racecars.

There were tests along the way and times where we were short on money. We found ourselves in the sleeper of our pickup truck on occasion. We reduced our racing in 1987 because of money problems, but I promised myself that I would never quit. I was a quitter in school and I didn't see things through, but I was nover going to quit this kid. I kept telling myself, "If I don't quit him, if I don't let him down, if I stay with this program, I think we're going to have us a race car driver." Who could have known that we were raising a three-time Winston Cup champion?

John Bickford and Claire B. Lang

Herman the German

I got the nickname "Herman the German" from a friend of my dad's named Bob Miller, a great guy. He was a big German man with a crew cut who ran the Central Auto Racing Association and owned a car lot that my father and I would visit. One day Bob tagged me "Herman the German," after a cartoon character in the local newspaper. I think it was because I was rebellious, hyper, and always in trouble. In school I would be getting thrown out for throwing paper wads or squeaking my chair, things like that.

As Rusty and Mike's younger brother, I got stepped on quite a few times, but I didn't complain because I didn't want to make waves. Sometimes I would suffer just so everybody else could have fun. Everyone always wanted me around because I was the life of the party. If somebody was getting together to have a party, or somebody needed something done to their racecar, they wanted me over.

A lot of people who hung around my brothers were real serious, so everyone always asked, "Where's Kenny?" I'm 36 now, and it wasn't until lately that I looked back and I realized just how innocent I was. I had this way--not by design--of getting along with people. I was the class clown in school and I always just liked having fun. When the Wallace's pulled into town, the first thing people asked was, "Where's Herman?" I was also the kid that absolutely drove you up the wall. I was diagnosed hyperactive, period, because I was always in trouble in school. They took me along to work on the racecars, but I just drove them crazy.

The Racing Family

In 1982, Rusty, Mike, and I were trying to figure out how to get me into racing and wondering where I'd fit in. Rusty knew he was going to be a racecar driver; Mike was racing for a hobby. I stayed busy being a mechanic and helping them with their racing careers.

One day, in Springfield, Illinois--a hundred miles up the road from where we lived in St. Louis--I got the opportunity to drive at the Street Stock State Championship race at the fairgrounds, a mile dirt track. It was an invitation-only race. There was a local champion around there named Pat Walsh, who had won everything. My brother, Mike, talked to him and said, "You know, Herm needs a break. What do you think about letting him drive that race?" To my surprise, he let me use his car! I took it to our shop and did some things to it aerodynamically. I filled in the front headlights and put a spoiler on the rear because it was a real fast racetrack. Then I went out there. My first time in a racecar against some two hundred cars, and I won the race! I could not believe it! I won the race! I thought I was the next Mario Andretti. I kept saying, "I told you! I told you I could do it!" My very first race ever and I won it and had never even driven a car before. I beat all these champions! But the strangest thing about it was that afterwards, I quit and went back to helping my brothers. I was so at peace with myself; I just wanted to let the family know that I could do it. So that was my first win. I still have the trophy and pictures. The most gratifying race for me came when I got the opportunity to help Rusty in 1998, at an event called the Bud Shootout. It was an all-star event made up of the 17 drivers who were the year's fastest qualifiers. It's a wide open event at the Daytona Speedway. You're willing to do whatever you have to do to win. It pays a lot of money--a couple hundred thousand dollars at that time--and whoever wins this race is "king" in Daytona for six or seven days.

So these 17 drivers lined up. I started eleventh or twelfth. I had a really good car and just took off when they dropped the green flag. I was in the draft there. I was just dicing and got up to around fourth when the caution flag fell. On the restarts, it's a double foul restart. Jeff Gordon was on the pole; my brother, Rusty, was on the outside. Jimmy Spencer was on the inside second row and I was on the outside second row. The rest of the field was behind us...good cars...Mark Martin...Schrader...good drivers. They dropped the green flag.

Well, Gordon missed his shift on the inside and Spencer barely missed him. It became a green and white-checkered race. We'd run all the laps. There was one lap left and it was a shootout. Spencer was on the inside and my brother on the outside. I'm looking at both of them and my first instinct was to cut low, make it three wide and cut by him. In the middle of turns one and two, we went up through the gearbox and I couldn't get underneath Spencer. I knew then that my best bet was to help my brother out, push him on past Spencer, and then I'd try to duke it out with Rusty. I had such a run on Rusty! I had my nose right up his rear. I had to let up on the gas because I was pushing so hard on his rear, that I was lifting his tail right off the ground! I had to modulate the throttle. I pushed him by Spencer, but as soon as Rusty got by him and took off, my car kind of stalled a little bit. Rusty had never won an event at Daytona until that day. The neatest thing about it all was that I knew that I helped Rusty win his very first event at Daytona. I realized that it was a pretty special deal. In every newspaper, there was a story about the brother act.

My father didn't race for a living but he should have. We raced every weekend and he won all the time. When you win a lot, you realize that people don't like you very much when you're having so much success. They're thinking, "Why can't it be us? Why can't we win?" Because my dad was so successful, it would be my mom and me, in the grandstands, defending my dad. I was not old enough to get in the pits, so we fought a lot protecting our ground.

When I was fifteen years old, we were in this restaurant in Fort Smith, Arkansas, after a race. We were borrowing this motor home from friends. We all just loaded it up and went racing. We owned the racecar, truck and trailer. So we're sitting there eating and towards the end of the meal, I told Don Kirn, one of the motormen, "I've got to go to the bathroom." You know, this is a fifteen-year-old kid telling a forty-year old man he's got to go to the bathroom, so he says, "Okay" and I go to the bathroom. When I came out of the restroom, there's nobody there and I start panicking. I run out to the front of the restaurant and they're gone. So I start walking; I think I'm just going to walk home. I don't know what comes over people when they panic at a young age, but I was just going to walk home. Then it dawned on me that I'm walking to Florida. So I went back to that restaurant and I called my mom and dad on the phone. Mom said "Oh, my god! It's okay, Kenny. Stay calm." Then they called the Arkansas Highway State Patrol and told them the whole story. So the highway patrol pulls over this whole caravan and they go to the motor home first. "Do you have a Rusty Wallace in here?" and Rusty says, "Yes, that's me." And they said, "Is your brother Kenny in here?" He of course answers, "Yeah, he's back in the hauler." So they go back in the hauler, which was carrying the racecar behind the motor home, and they ask, "Is Kenny in here?" and they say, "No, he's up in the motor home." Well, they knew then that it was bad news. At the time, it was a tragedy. They sent someone from Springfield, Missouri, to Fort Smith to pick me up, but by the time I caught up to them in Springfield, Rusty was mad at me because it delayed them some eight hours. Two or three days later, when we all gathered around, everyone wanted to know what the hell happened. I said, "I'll tell you exactly what happened. I went into that bathroom and I had to go number two and sat down. Have you ever been on one of those toilet seats and the toilet paper roll won't let the toilet paper off?" I gnawed on that toilet paper roll like a gerbil trying to get that stuff off. It probably took me five minutes or longer to wipe! To this day every time I go to the bathroom the people that know me say, "Make sure that toilet paper roll is good or we're gonna leave you!"

The biggest thing I learned from racing is how to deal with people from everywhere--Daytona Beach, Florida, to Calgary, Canada, and even Japan. My mom and dad didn't have money to help me start racing. Racing taught me that if you want to do something that takes money, you've got to go get the money. That's the hardest thing about racing. You've got to become a salesman if you want to be a racecar driver. Family has been and still is the most important thing in my life. I couldn't have done it without my family.

When I first met my wife, Kim, I was a pest. I had

a thing for good-looking girls. We met in photography class; I was a senior and she was a junior. Everyone was in their seats; she and her sister, Kelly, were late. Kim had a great body, a dark tan, white teeth--she's still a knockout today. When I first saw her, my jaw hit the floor. I just stared at her. We had to develop film in the darkroom and I decided I would try my hardest to get in that dark room to start flirting with her. The problem was that Kim was about sixteen going on twenty-five. She's always been very mature, always made the right decisions, and always made good grades. She didn't go for any of this flirting around stuff at that time. One of her friends came to me and said, "Kim Poole wants to go out with you."

I said, "Well she is a big flirt and a tease and I ain't going out with her." But I had a big crush on her. She was just so mature and I was so silly, wanting to have fun. I was rambunctious and she just constantly had it together. It really bugged me. After the semester ended, about a month or two later, I walked out of that classroom and, lo and behold I got this phone call. It was Kim. I was working on the racecourse at the time. I'll never forget the words she said, "Kenny Wallace?" I told her that I was Kenny Wallace, to which she replied, "Well, is it a crime to want to go out with you?" As of June 23, 2000, we've been married for 16 years. We'd been going out since '81 and got married in '84. We had Brooke two years later.

I think when you're a new husband and you've got a daughter coming along, you're into playing this father role. You go into that delivery room and it's obviously the most amazing thing in life--to think that there is a "you" in a belly! When I was in there to actually take part and see the whole delivery, it was the biggest thing in my life. The first birth and my first win. I can tell you after they were all done, they were both just total relief. I just wanted to sit down and relax and thank God that everything turned out real well. The first birth was fine; I actually watched everything; the second and third kids were C-sections. I was a big supporter of Kim. But when she chewed on a wet washcloth, it reminded me of Richard Petty, because he used to chew on a wet washcloth during a race.

I now have three lovely daughters, but there are huge differences in them. Brooke is a carbon copy of her mother. She's got a dark tan and is very, very mature. She gets "A's" in school, just like Kim did. I can embarrass her in a heartbeat. "Brooke," I say, "Give me a kiss," and she'll get stiff and say, "Dad!" It could just be her and me in the middle of the woods and I can still embarrass her. She's a sweetheart and she's a lot of fun. She was the funniest when she was a kid. We would sit around the house and watch videotapes--that's a big pastime, just get out tapes from ten years ago. Brandy--the middle one--she's our entertainment. Brandy is our tomboy, but about a year ago, she surprised us all and turned into a girl. I guess that was from going to school and all of a sudden seeing boys. A few years ago, when she was a tomboy, she wanted to race. We bought her this small car--a Bandelarro, to race over at the Charlotte Motor Speedway. About $30,000 later, I was head over heels about this Bandelarro. When she was eleven, she was racing it and this forty-year-old guy she was racing hit her in the left rear quarter-panel and got her into the wall. When the wreck was over, her eyes were about the size of silver dollars and she did not want to race anymore. So, I sold everything and now Brandy is our softball player. Our last daughter, Brittany, is a carbon copy of me. She's all girl, a sweetheart who doesn't want to hurt anybody's feelings. She can be a character, though. She'll say something and I'll ask, "Did that came out of your mouth?" By the time we had Brittany, I was cocky; I thought I was Mr. Dad. As I was standing behind the sheet with Kim in the delivery room, I got the great idea that I'd watch this baby be taken out of her belly. Ohmigod! There's just nothing that can compare to cutting a belly open and seeing another human being inside the belly. It was amazing. I about fainted. They stopped the procedures real quick, snapped sauce on me, put me down on a stretcher and a gurney. So, birth is amazing; it's out-of-hand and it's also scary. But you know, so is life.

Kenny Wallace and Ron Camacho

Tell Her With "Taters"

I know Momma, the late Eula Faye Marlin, was dead set against me racing the big tracks. They just scared her. She didn't particularly like her husband racing on them, and she sure as heck didn't want her son racing on them.

But I was a racer and Daddy knew that. If I was going to race Winston Cup, I was going to be spending some time at Talladega. That's all there was to it. So, we got everything ready to go and knew we were going. We'd done everything but tell Momma. Daddy said, "Let me handle it. Don't say nothing." So I kept quiet.

We were sitting there at dinner one night and I guess he figured out this was the time to do it. He was spearing a piece of meat and looking away from her, and he said, "Pass them taters there, Eula Faye. Sterling's running at Talladega." Course, she had pretty well figured it out by then and I don't think it was a big surprise. She still wasn't too happy about it, but I think she figured there wasn't much she could do about it either.

Now that my son, Steadman, has gotten a taste for this stuff, he's going to be wanting to move up one of these days, too.

I know that my wife, Paula, knows that. And I know down deep in my heart that I'm going to have to lay it out to her one of these days, too, and I'll probably do it just like Daddy and Momma... with "taters."

Sterling Marlin and Claire B. Lang

Take Care of My Mother

Steve Park was the new driver of the Pennzoil car, owned by Dale Earnhardt Inc., and I was his new motor coach driver. Two weeks before the accident happened, I asked him the question that I dreaded. "What do you want me to do in case you're in a bad crash?" He knew exactly what I was asking and answered without hesitation, "Sign me into the hospital and take care of my mother."

There was something else that stands out now that I look back. I'll never forget him walking into the motor home the week before the accident. We were at Las Vegas on Saturday and he didn't make the race. I told him that he was going to have to go through tougher times than this to be able to appreciate the good times in his career. Can you believe that? Little did we know how much those words would ring true. The very next week, on March 6, 1998, we were at Atlanta Motor Speedway with six minutes left in practice. He took the car out for one more run and that's when it happened-- the crash into pit wall. He had a broken femur, broken right shoulder blade, left collarbone, and broken teeth.

It really hit me when his mom and dad got to the hospital, because all he kept saying to me as he was going into surgery was, "Please, whatever you do, take care of my mother." He said it probably 25 times before he went into surgery. His father, Bob, and his mom, Dottie, are like his best friends.

They flew him back to the hospital in Charlotte. When he was discharged, they backed the ambulance right up to the garage door of his house. They had a wheel chair waiting there, inside the garage. Steve was barely out of the ambulance when he took one look at it and said, "I am not going to be in a wheel chair." His mind was made up. I stayed with him during the day and his mother stayed with him at night for months.

The doctors didn't want him out and about at all, but when he'd been home only two weeks he decided that he wanted to go to the Bristol race--not to drive, just to be there. I had to go ask Dale and Theresa Earnhardt if he could go. Dale told me he could, but that I'd better stay with him because if anybody hit that leg and injured Park again, it was going to be my rear end. You can bet I looked out for Steve on that trip.

By the grace of God, and his own determination and faith, he was going to get back in that racecar that season. I would never have believed it, but I saw it with my own eyes. I've never watched anybody in my life work as hard as he did in rehab. It's just unbelievable the pain he endured and how hard he pushed himself. You could see the tears in his eyes; that's how hard he worked to get back.

I'll never forget the doctor telling Steve's mom and dad and me, after they did the surgery that Saturday morning after the crash, that if he even walked in a year, it would be by the grace of God. Walk-heck! He drove! He was back in his car racing in five months at the Brickyard in August of '98.

One of the best memories of my life will always be when Steve won his first Winston Cup race on August 13, 2000 at Watkins Glen. He parked his car on the start-finish line and paid tribute to the fans by jumping on top of it. I remember thinking, "This is not only a race win; it is a victory of the human spirit."

Eddie Jarvis and Claire B. Lang

Passing Along a Tradition

Racing has been my family and my family has been racing my whole life. It's a tradition and a legacy. A lot of people think of racing's roots and immediately think of the South. They think about the Pettys and the Allisons. But in Michigan, where I grew up, I know families that raced their whole lives.

I'm a third generation driver. My grandfather, Wilson Fedewa, and grandmother drove, too. They started out in the 40's racing motorcycles on flat tracks and fairgrounds. Grandma was his crew chief and raced a few times in one of his cars. I always thought that was pretty cool. I have pictures of her wearing her helmet. In the 1940's, several of the ladies who followed their husbands raced.

Grandpa loved to race. He was a machinist by trade, but didn't make much money. To supplement their income, they made their own parachutes and jumped out of hot air balloons at fairs. It was pretty amazing stuff! They would do a little trapeze act up on the balloons, then parachute down.

Grandpa helped me build my first racecar out in his garage in 1985. It was a dirt car he bought for me and we fixed it up. I was very fortunate that I had that quality time with him when we built that car. As a teenager, you take your grandparents for granted. I think I did, anyway. You go over to their house; you're in and out, you say, "Hi!" and "Bye!" and maybe eat lunch. But you don't really sit down and appreciate them. You don't believe anyone is ever going to leave you. Grandpa died later that year. Grandma died four or five years after that.

Racing is important to me but it's not as important as having my loved ones healthy. Last year, my mom was diagnosed with lung cancer. She had half a lung removed. It was a major operation and a severe reality check. When your parents get sick--and both of mine have been very sick, (my dad had open-heart surgery and then my mom last year with this lung cancer), it really hits home. Mom's operation went on while I was racing in Atlanta.

When you get in the racecar you don't think about outside things. My thoughts are on life. The opposite of life is death, and when you're young, you don't think about losing your family and you take things for granted. When you get a few years under your belt, you soon realize that life does come to an end and you start taking your parents and the things you do and want to accomplish a little more seriously. The day of Mom's operation was tough, but as a driver you're a trained athlete. You can't have those thoughts inside your head when you get in the car. If I did, I'd pull it in. Dad raced everything. He started out racing the local tracks, winning several hundred features around Michigan. Behind the wheel, he's probably the hardest racing man I've ever seen. He literally rode the wheels off the car! My uncle Gary, who was racing about the same time, was at the other end of the spectrum. He was smooth and tactical and won a lot of races. I came up somewhere in between.

Grandpa was inducted into the Michigan Motor Sports Hall of Fame when I was 16. Dad and Uncle Gary got inducted at the same time in 1985. At that age, I was more interested in girls, my racing career, and having fun. I didn't appreciate those important moments. As I've grown older, I've started to appreciate what the three of them have accomplished. They were first-class people. They didn't make it into the Hall of Fame by winning one race; they were inducted because they where all first-class people-- aside from the fact that they could drive a racecar. They handled their careers treating people the way they wanted to be treated.

When I started racing, my dad had just retired, but I did race my uncle on several occasions. My cousin Tommy, who was a few years younger than I, also started racing about the same time. I am lucky I got to race my dad, my uncle, and my cousin in several exhibition races; like the Father and Son races at the Spartan Racetrack in Michigan. Dad and I, Tommy and Uncle Gary, and my cousin teamed up to race in these old street stocks. People were nice enough to let us use their cars, and we just tore the heck out of them! I think Gary won by default. The rest of us were sitting on the infield because we'd been so determined to beat our dads and cousin that we all ran into each other!

I've been fortunate to have friends as well as family with me throughout my career. My friend Bryan Smith's dad was my dad's crew chief when he first started racing. The two of them grew up in the same neighborhood; just like Bryan and I grew up together at the track and still work together.

As soon as I was old enough to drive, Dad bought me a car and Bryan became my...well, we didn't know what to call the position back then. He was my buddy. So Bryan has been with me on and off throughout my career from the late models to the ARTGO circuit up into the ARCA series now in NASCAR's Busch series. He's worked for some other teams, but we always seem to come back together.

In 1995, we won our first race with Bryan as the crew chief. Everybody who worked on that car came with me from Michigan to follow our dream of racing. My first win at the Nazareth Speedway meant more to me than all of the others combined. We had a real bunch of talented, determined racers. Scott Diehl, who worked on my car, is now the car chief for Tony Stewart.

Racing is the only thing I've ever known. I don't know what I'd do if I couldn't drive a racecar and had to get a regular job. It's an ego thing. I really don't care about the money, but I sure like walking into the garage area knowing that I've beat everyone else! It's the best feeling in the world!

It's all about tradition. It's in your blood. One of my most vivid memories is from when I was 17 and Bryan and I were building that car with my grandfather. We had already raced on Friday that weekend and needed to run to the parts store to get some things for Saturday night's race. We took my dad's car, a beautiful brand new silver Thunderbird.

We were eyeballing some girls at the stoplight. When the light turned green, they took off and so did I. Unfortunately, the car in front of me didn't. I rear-ended it, wrecking my dad's brand new car. When I came home, I parked in the weeds in front of the fencerow so that the front end was hidden. Grandpa was in the garage. A little later, he came to me and asked, "Do you think your dad won't notice it because you parked it like that?"

I braced myself for the lecture, but it never came. Instead, all I could see was a man trying his best to hold back a grin. Half frightened and confused, I summoned up the courage to say, "I'm not sure." He thought that was the funniest thing he'd ever heard! I later learned that when my dad was 15, Grandpa and Grandma left town for the weekend, leaving behind their pride and joy '55 Chevy--a streetcar. Dad took it and gutted it, then drove it to the racetrack. That's why Grandpa was smiling. I'll never forget that look! It had taken a few years, but he'd finally gotten his justice! He didn't want to tell me he was happy, but I guarantee my dad took a razzing about it. He had just passed down another tradition!

Tim Fedewa and Ron Camacho

Preparing For The Ultimate Healing

The sun warmed the April morning air that felt fresh and crisp against my face as I walked from the parking lot to the rocking chair lined front porch of the familiar Cracker Barrel restaurant at exit 36. I come here every Tuesday morning at 8:00, go immediately to the round table that sits alone in a corner just as you enter the dining area. It is here at this table that a small group meets each week to discuss some of life's most important issues. It is so routine that I can predict each week the arrival of each person and what they do and where they will sit. Ronnie Stevens, a businessman connected with racing, has been at the table for probably half an hour already reading the newspaper and having a cup of coffee. I arrive next and join him, sitting to his right. Moments later, Michael Waltrip, a NASCAR race driver and his dad, Leroy, will enter. Michael sits to my right and Leroy heads to the men's room before seating himself next to Ronnie. Moments later, Buffy, Michael's wife, and Dana, Michael's niece, arrive to fill in the remaining seats at the table.

This Tuesday morning was just different. I knew that Ronnie would not be there. I sat on the long, narrow front porch in one of the many rocking chairs, enjoying the morning sun as it beamed directly on me. It was a wonderful morning in all its glory. I sat, waiting for the others to arrive. Much to my amazement, Leroy drove up all by himself. I was really surprised, as Leroy had all but given up on driving and the others in the family would not let him drive. I figured that he must have sneaked off without the others knowing about his driving to the Cracker Barrel that morning.

"Good Morning," Leroy greeted me with a sheepish smile. "Michael is out of town and Buffy and Dana can't come this morning, so I just drove myself down today. I guess it's just you and me." We walked in together to our usual round table in the corner. In our life issue studies, we had been discussing some things about life after death. After we made our usual order and said our "Howdys!" to the waitress, Leroy spoke out quickly about what was on his mind, "You know I've got lots of questions about this dying thing. Max, you have been my teacher. I need to know how to get through with this dying thing. I want to know all I can about what the Bible says about dying, about heaven. I just have lots of questions." I was sensitive to Leroy's need, knowing that he had been battling cancer for sometime. We began to discuss the reality of death and the hope of eternal life with God. We talked about his fears. Even though it was just the two of us, this meeting changed the setting for the group discussions for the next eight months.

Tuesdays became a more meaningful experience to the group, as we all joined in with helping Leroy prepare for death. We talked about the fears of the unknown, comparisons of birth and death, life after death and, most of all, preparations. It was a time that we all looked forward to with great anticipation as we engaged with Leroy in the planning of his departure and the discovery that death for a believer in Christ is really ultimate healing. One day Leroy asked, "Max, will you help me plan my funeral? I don't want a lot of crying. I want it to be happy." I sat with him to outline the service that some day would come. He was pleased with our plans.

Tuesday, January 11, was the crowning day of all

our meetings. Early that morning I caught a plane from West Palm Beach, Florida, to rush to the Cracker Barrel gathering. I knew that Leroy would not be at this meeting. He had been hospitalized and returned home much too weak for the trip to exit 36. I had tried to reach Michael on Monday to see if we could meet with Leroy at the house instead. Upon my arrival in Charlotte, Missy, my executive assistant, called me to say that Michael had just called and that Leroy had had a bad night and was not doing well. Before I could call Michael, he called me to say that Leroy had quietly slipped into the presence of God. He died peacefully, knowing that all was well with God. He had given evidence of that throughout our meetings.

Wednesday, January 12, we gathered at the First Baptist Church of Mooresville, NC, to celebrate Leroy's life and his crowning day. With two popular drivers in the family, the church was filled with family, friends, and those from the racing community. Leroy had been a part of the NASCAR scene since Darrell's entry into the sport in the mid-seventies. The memorial service was very different. It literally was a happy occasion. It was carried out just as Leroy had planned. Darrell shared some fond memories of his dad. Ronnie Stevens talked about the Tuesday meetings at the Cracker Barrel. Michael spoke of Leroy's fifty years of marriage to Margaret, his love of golf, his dressing like at man in GQ and his love for God. He shared this quote from C. S. Lewis, "If I cannot find the things in this world that will fulfill my deepest longings, then perhaps I am made for a different world."

Leroy entered that different world--a world without sickness or pain. We all joined in the celebration of Leroy's ultimate healing. People left that day different-

-different because Leroy's plans gave cause for celebration and a different view of dying.

Max Helton

Staying in Touch

Our family has always been close. The Pettys have lived in the same community for years and certainly all my life. My mom and dad have always lived close to my grandparents, my uncles, and cousins. We have all been in racing together. My grandfather was a racer and racing has been all that our family has known. We have always been one big family and we share our lives with each other.

In my junior high school years, my parents enrolled me in a basketball camp at Elon College near Burlington, North Carolina. My mom wanted to hear from me each day that I was going to be gone, so she bought post cards and put stamps on them. She had one for each day that I was to be gone, expecting me to write her each day giving her details of life at the camp. Mom packed them away into my bags. She told me about them as she dropped me off for my week of basketball camp.

My mom left and I went into my room and got the cards out and took them to the nearest mailbox. I took all the stamped post cards and put them in the mailbox, writing on only one of them.

In a couple of days, my mom went to her mailbox and received all of the stamped post cards at one time with only one having a single line on it. This is not what she had in mind as a way of staying in touch. I thought it was funny--my mom didn't.

Kyle Petty and Max Helton

CHAPTER THREE
Racing With Faith

"Courage is fear that has said its prayers ."
Karle Baker

An Unexpected Alliance

The atmosphere was electric in Atlanta! Three NASCAR drivers (Mark Martin, Dale Jarrett, and Jeff Gordon) had the chance to win the Winston Cup championship this Sunday in the last race of the season. The "hype" was extraordinary all weekend, as seldom in the history of racing have three people been in the position to win a championship with only one race left in the season. The championship is the highest achievement for any driver for the entire year. It certainly was a momentous occasion for these three men. It was a special weekend for thousands of NASCAR fans.

During the day on Saturday, as these drivers were hounded by the media for stories, the most remarkable story was forming quietly between those three drivers and me. A special meeting was being planned that would occur following the usual Saturday Bible study that met in Mark's motor coach in the infield area reserved for the drivers and owners.

Shortly after 7:30 p.m. everyone leaves the study except Mark, Dale, Jeff and me. What was about to happen probably had never happened in the history of racing. In fact, it probably had not happened in any major sport on the eve of a championship game. Seldom would any professional athlete commune with their opponents in any kind of setting. But here in the quietness of Mark Martin's motor coach this unique experience was unfolding.

After we chatted a moment, Mark Martin,

76

unquestionably one of the toughest racecar drivers ever; Dale Jarrett, who came from a racing pedigree; and Jeff Gordon, loved and hated for the absolute dominance he brought to racing, joined me in holding hands for a special time of prayer.

Dale started the prayer, asking God for safety and to give Mark and Jeff a good day of racing that would be fun and exciting. Mark prayed expressing thanks for allowing him to be in the position for the championship with these drivers, and for God's graciousness for giving him the privilege to race. Jeff began to communicate his gratitude to God and how much He meant to him and that God would allow each of the drivers to be at their best and not have any difficulties during the race. They were united in their prayers--"We give this race to you, God."

Max Helton

Broken to Become Beautiful

Our spotter said, "Spin on the backstretch!" When I heard the Motor Racing Network announce that Jeff Purvis was involved, I realized Andy had been close to him in the pack. Still, after the announcement, neither our spotter nor Andy said anything in the minutes after the accident. When Andy didn't come around to the pit we radioed him. I'll never forget the tone of his voice; it sounded weak and distant, as if every breath was being fought for. When he came back over the radio he sounded as if he were a hundred miles away, "The car is junk. My leg hurts real bad."

It was the 1999 Busch Series season-opening race at Daytona International Speedway and Andy had qualified in the first round. Andy and his team were looking forward to a strong sophomore season after winning the "Rookie of the Year" Championship in their freshman year. I hugged Andy especially tight that day and put him in the racecar with a "Go get 'em!" kiss, and then I walked to my post on top of the pit cart. After the command to start the engines, I emphasized the "be safe" part of my traditional affirmation. The risk of injury and death is something the wife of a racecar driver lives with daily. You know it can happen, it's always in the back of your mind, but you never consciously think it can happen to you and you secretly pray every night that is doesn't.

For the last five years, after the command, "Gentlemen, Start your engines!" I would support my husband by whispering, "Good luck! Be Safe! I love you!" into the radio. I'm not sure why I began saying it, maybe to quiet my own fears or perhaps it was to make these the last sentiments he would hear from me in case of injury...or worse.

At the same moment, as Andy's words came over the radio, the TV camera focused on what was left of my husband's car. For the first time in my life, I knew sheer terror. Everything, my entire life and my future, was sitting in a heap of twisted metal. I began running to the infield care center to meet Andy because it was the only helpful thing I could do. My fears must have been written on my face in those first moments that seemed like a tortuous eternity. As Michael Waltrip and Jeff Purvis got out of the ambulance they immediately began assuring me that Andy was all right. I wanted to believe them. But I needed to see for myself that my husband was "there."

The overwhelming feeling of strength that I felt through the ordeal was amazing. No matter who you are, somewhere in your soul and in the back of your mind you always wonder how you will react should something bad ever happen to someone you love. Now as the ambulance came closer, I anxiously stood waiting...waiting to know how severe my husband's injuries were after a terrifying multi-car crash at a 190 miles an hour.

It took me back to another time that Andy had endured in his life. Andy had contracted Guillian Barre Syndrome, a virus that attacks the central nervous and muscular systems. He was hospitalized for 87 days in 1988 at age 19. During this period his nervous system shut down, his lungs collapsed and he was left paralyzed. Andy has the ability to endure immense pain without uttering a complaint and that's what was scary. To hear him say that his leg was "hurt bad" and to hear the raw pain in his voice, I knew that he was truly in agony.

Now laying on the ambulance gurney, a lopsided grin and a teasing comment assured me that Andy was okay. The feeling of helplessness, of not knowing what to do, frustrates and saddens your spirit. You are wishing that you could do anything to help to take the pain away. If I could have just traded places with him, I'd have done it in a heartbeat.

For twelve hours a day, during the week that Andy was in the hospital, we received many cards, flowers, and gifts, not only from friends and fans, but also fellow drivers. The experience was humbling. Adam Petty, Randy LaJoie and Todd Bodine, among others, were all so supportive. These expressions show what a close-knit community exists between the drivers and the teams. Even with the amount of competition that the drivers have to maintain, racing to win, there is a love and respect that they have toward each other.

Andy and I began asking God to show us where He fits into our lives. After everything Andy's been through we realize that there aren't any sure answers, but we trust that one day there will be. We wondered if God were trying to tell us to leave racing, so we prayed about what to do.

The next morning I received a "Daily Fax" at work. I am usually too busy to take the time to read it. But on this day I did. It was a Divine postcard. It was a story about the building of the Iranian Royal Palace in Tehran. The story told of the architect's wish to hang huge sheets of mirrors on the walls. When the mirrors arrived from Paris, they were shattered. After the architect's anger cleared, he ordered all the broken pieces collected; then he smashed them into tiny pieces and glued them to the walls to become a silvery shimmering mosaic.

Broken to become beautiful!
It's possible to turn your scars to stars.
It's possible to be better because of the brokenness.
Never, never underestimate His power to repair and restore!

In those closing remarks, Andy and I found our answer.

By Susan Santerre

Intimidation Inspiration

Dale Earnhardt's career made a great impression on me during a very difficult time in my life. My parents' health was declining and they moved from Pennsylvania to Virginia to be closer to their children. My father was a retired machinist, a tough World War II tank division commander who, in his younger days, loved to race. He was well known in our hometown for his love of the sport and his superb engine-building abilities. Dad always hoped that my brother and I would also become interested in racing. To encourage it, every Friday night he would take us to the local track.

In late 1996, Dad's wish came true. At the time, I was not a NASCAR fan and knew little about the sport. However, I inexplicably began getting a strong impression to pray for Dale Earnhardt. Being a Christian, I took this very seriously. Since I knew little about him, I began reading everything I could so I would be able to pray more effectively. As I shared this information with Dad, it kindled a relationship between us that I will always treasure. Dad was ecstatic that I was finally interested in the sport he so loved. He opened up and began sharing many of his racing experiences, helping my brother and me to better understand what was happening on race day.

Our family started to seriously delve into NASCAR. Every weekend, we'd go to Dad's and watch the race with him. This soon became the highlight of his week. The 1997 Daytona 500 was one of the first races we saw together. Dad loved to hear the latest on what I had learned about Dale, and this race proved to be an excellent example of seeing some of Dale's well-known tributes put into action. Dad admired men who had a never-give-up attitude. He soon witnessed Dale's tenacity and greatly respected him for it.

Near the end of the race, Dale crashed and rolled his #3 car. We all watched the accident with dismay and disappointment, hoping Dale was all right and sorry that his day was over. The television cameras showed Dale climbing out of the car and being led to a waiting ambulance. A few minutes later, Dale emerged from the ambulance and returned to his wrecked vehicle. "That's unheard of!" Dad exclaimed, with a slight smile. "I wonder what he's doing."

What was he up to? Dale had seen a crew member start up his #3 car to haul it away and he wasn't about to let that happen. Now he motioned the guy out of the car, then climbed in himself, with no helmet. Dad started to chuckle. His admiration of this man was growing by the second.

Dale returned to the track and finished the race in spite of his wrecked car. Dad was tickled pink. He loved to see a man with the grit and guts to finish a race "come hell or high water." It was exactly the attitude he'd tried to instill in us as we were growing up. I remember him telling me, "Kid, no matter what is going on around you or how bad things seem to be, you never just sit there feeling sorry for yourself. That will get you nowhere in life. You get up, and keep on going. You finish what you set out to do, no matter what anyone else thinks."

After the race finished, Dad grinned at me and again emphasized, "This is the attitude we need to have in our day-to-day experiences." I would later use this same example to encourage Dad as things in his life began to slide downhill.

That same year, we also attended a few Winston Cup races, where we were lucky enough to meet Dale. Each time, we rushed back to tell Dad about our experiences. He'd always get a kick out of them.

One story Dad particularly enjoyed was when we left the Martinsville race to drive to Dale Earnhardt's Chevrolet dealership where Dale was signing autographs. Although we had been warned that Dale was not very personable, we didn't find that to be the case. The same rainstorm that had forced the delay of the Martinsville race delayed Dale's arrival at the dealership. As we pulled in the lot, there was talk of cutting off the autograph line. However, when word of it reached Dale, he stopped what he was doing, looked outside at the people who had gathered, then told his staff he would stay and sign autographs until every last fan had been through the line. He didn't have to do that, but he did and my respect for him grew. When it was our turn to meet him, he was very kind and listened to what we had to say. Dad was so happy we were able to meet him and clearly loved hearing about Dale's flexibility in the midst of a hectic schedule.

On another occasion, we were visiting my brother in Charlotte, North Carolina, when we learned that the "Intimidator" prototype Monte Carlo was on display at Dale's dealership. We decided to go there to see the car. When we arrived, we noticed a crowd of people gathered inside a large tent set up on the lot. My husband and two sons immediately headed for the showroom to see the car, but I stayed outside, curious about what was going on inside the tent. When I asked a fellow spectator, I learned that Dale was there signing autographs. I grabbed my camera and bought some

Goodwrench bio cards; then went to the showroom to get my husband and sons. Each of us was only allowed one autograph. As we waited, my husband gave his card to a man whose little girl had nothing for Dale to sign. As we moved through the line, Dale signed our cards, speaking to each us. When he saw my husband had nothing for him to sign, Dale just reached up and autographed his t-shirt. "That shirt now belongs to me," I jokingly told my husband, who said he knew as soon as Dale signed it that it would be the last time he'd ever be able to wear it. When he got home and regaled Dad with the story, he laughed and laughed, glad Dale had accommodated everyone.

Dale's racing abilities were the topic of many fun conversations between Dad and me. He loved the man's tenacity and perseverance. As a veteran of many World War II battles, Dad understood what it meant to race against time. I began realizing as the year progressed, how much of himself Dad was revealing to me, and how precious to me that sharing was.

In early 1998, sunny times seemed few and far between. Mom was now in a nursing home, her health deteriorating daily. Dad was bedridden with heart problems and terribly depressed. We were all looking forward to the start of the next racing season. Dad knew I was praying for Dale to win a Daytona 500 and he sure wanted to see that happen, too. On January 23, we watched NASCAR's 50th Anniversary television special with Dad. The show featured historic tracks, including the Langhorne Speedway in Pennsylvania. When Dad saw the aerial view, he told us he used to race on the circular dirt track and often brought his father along so he could watch the race. He laughed as he recalled how appalled Grandma was because Grandpa came home dirtier than Dad. Until he told us, I had no idea he'd ever raced there. Little did I know that as we listened to Dad's stories and watched the special, that it would be the last time I would ever see him alive. Right after that visit, he suffered a relapse and was admitted to the hospital. When he was released, he went home and passed away.

The Sunday of the Daytona 500, my husband and sons joined me in Dad's empty house to watch the race, just as we had done in the past. I could still see him in the bed and hear our talks as the race progressed. It was so hard not being able to reach out to touch him. So many things passed through my mind. Would I be able to handle all the extra responsibilities as executor of Dad's estate? I worried about my mother's failing health, knowing Dad's death might also push her over the edge. And I kept thinking about all the things about Dale that Dad and I discussed, especially how he'd hang in there, get up and keep on going no matter what.

Suddenly, I was jerked back to reality. Dale was leading the race! I stood up behind Dad's favorite chair and began praying. "Lord," I said, "I need Dale to win. If he can win the Daytona 500 after all this time, never having given up, then, Lord, I know that I can grit my teeth and move forward and make it."

Tears were streaming down my face. I couldn't stop them. Dale was the front-runner! He was winning! I could almost see Dad smiling and felt him sharing in my joy. By now, all four of us were on our feet, jumping up and down and screaming. He did it! Dale did it! And I knew then that I'd make it, too.

Kathy Nelson

Forgiveness

Darrell Waltrip and Ricky Craven had wrecked each other near the end of the fall race at Charlotte. At the next race (Rockingham) as the last laps wound down, the same two racers collided again on the track. Darrell was angered at Ricky as he walked hastily toward his team's transporter. I had never seen Darrell so angry and I was concerned that he might do something that he would later regret. As I entered the lounge of the transporter, he threw his helmet down in anger and disgust. I walked up to him, got in his face and said, "Darrell hit me!" He started smiling and said, "Max, I can't hit you." I knew it was working and was glad that he didn't hit me. After we chatted a moment, he settled down and I moved on to see Ricky.

Ricky was very troubled about the events. He expressed his deep regards and respect for Darrell. We chatted some and I left.

At the Winston Cup chapel services, the drivers participate in the service by opening the service, leading in prayer, and reading the Bible. The next race was at Phoenix. Jeff Gordon was set up to open the service with Michael Waltrip leading the opening prayer. The chapel service is always conducted immediately following the drivers' meeting.

After the drivers' meeting, I saw Michael talking to Jeff and overheard him whisper, "I can't pray today. I have laryngitis." No problem! Jeff knew that he could always call on Lake Speed or Darrell Waltrip on the spur of the moment. (They had agreed to always be ready.)

After Jeff welcomed everyone to the morning

service and made a few announcements, he calls on Darrell to pray. Darrell slowly walks to the pulpit and says, "I can't pray because I have something in my heart against Ricky Craven." Wow! That certainly got everyone's attention, especially Ricky's, who was sitting in the service along with most of the drivers and team members.

Suddenly you could hear a pin drop (this is in the midst of Sunday morning's busy garage activities). Darrell continued as the crowd eagerly awaited his words, "Ricky come up here." Ricky walked cautiously to the front to be met by Darrell's outstretched arms. They embraced and Darrell asked for forgiveness. With Ricky in his arms, Darrell prayed.

It was one of the most moving experiences in my many years of ministry. There was hardly a dry eye among them.

Max Helton

Front Row Joe

How did I get the name "Front Row Joe?"--From Wally Dallenbach, my 1997 teammate. He tossed me the nickname when we were at Pocono. At the time, Wally had been running real well and was on the pole in qualifying. During a pre race interview, he glanced my way, grinned, and said, "Don't count out Ol' 'Front Row Joe.'" When I beat him out for the pole, the name stuck.

Racing has always been a family thing for me, starting back with the tool-and-die shop our family owned when I was growing up in Lakeland, Florida. Having the machine shop really helped me out with my racing. One of the gifts God gave me was the ability to look at something, and then figure out right away how to make it better. In the early days, I did almost all of the work myself, but I also had guys who would work with me part-time, helping out after their day jobs.

I got my first motorcycle in 1975 when I was 12. I saw a motorcross race on TV. Back then, "Hurricane" Bob Hannah was the guy to beat. I will never forget sitting in front of the TV in our living room, watching these guys going over big jumps, flying high in the air. I told my parents, "One of these days, I'm going to do that!" It took me a little while to convince them, but pretty soon, I had my motorcycle. We had ten acres surrounding the family business, so I set up a practice track right there. That was where I got interested in racing for the first time. I got on my motorcycle and made it do some pretty crazy things. I remember this one stunt in particular. There was a mound of dirt that had been dumped on our property. I figured out if I could hit that thing doing 40 mph, I would fly through the air. When I got it worked out, I invited Mom and Dad to come watch me. They thought I was nuts!

Shortly after that, I started racing and I've been racing something ever since. When I got my first bike I wanted to figure out how to do the best I could, so I went and raced against guys who had better and faster equipment. I was amazed to discover I could run pretty well with them. My next step was a better bike. Then, instead of running third every week, I started smoking those same guys! At one point in time, I was racing everything and riding in four classes: 80 hp, 100 hp, 125 hp, and 250 hp.

At the end of the 1986 season, I decided to switch to cars. I got started in mini stocks. I went to the junkyard and bought an old Ford Pinto, put a roll cage in it, rebuilt the motor and went racing. The following year, we rebuilt a Scirocco and ran a bunch of races in Lakeland and Auburndale, Florida. I won a lot of races in both cars. At the end of that first year, I had won 50 races and decided it was time to get into late models. We found a good deal on a late model car and went racing in Florida. In 1990, we moved up from late models to the NASCAR Busch series. It was a struggle in the beginning because we'd run well for a while, but it seemed we could never really finish well. It took getting used to new cars, new tracks, new everything. In 1991, it got easier and we ran pretty decent. We started getting poles and won two or three races. Then, in 1992, we won the NASCAR Busch Series Championship. The following year, we were pretty much at the pack the whole time. When we jumped into Winston Cup in '94, we had to start all over again because the "Cup" competition is tough, really tough.

When I first came into NASCAR, Dale Earnhardt looked out for me and our families became friends. He understood what we were trying to do. In the early '90's, we would sit at his farm, drink Sundrop, talk racing, and just have a good time. Then there was Darryl Waltrip; I knew all the Waltrips from back when I was racing against them in the Busch series. They're all great competitors. Donny Allison has helped, too. Both he and Bobby Allison were very inspiring to me when I was growing up.

The hardship the Allison family has endured has affected the whole racing community. Deep down, you know it hurts their team and their family much more than it does the rest of us, but we know how they feel. My family went through it in March, 1997, when my 27-year-old brother, John, died from head injuries five days after he crashed into the outside retaining wall at the Homestead Motorsports Complex during a NASCAR truck series race. John was the Truck series' first casualty. So many drivers have been getting killed lately--Adam Petty, now Kenny Irwin. Drivers don't usually get killed this often, but in the last few years, it's been getting worse. You never think anything bad can happen, but when it did, I still wanted to continue racing. It was something John and I had talked about before. We agreed that if either one of us got hurt, the other one had to keep going. He loved to race and I do, too, so I kept going. If it were the other way around, I would have expected him to keep going, too. My mother asked me to stop racing because she didn't want another son getting hurt. I promised her I would be extra safe, but that I had to keep doing what I wanted to do. She finally accepted my decision.

My faith helped me deal with these tragedies. I grew up in a Catholic environment; I attended Catholic grade school and high school. I believe in God. When I was growing up, I went to church on Sundays and learned about the Lord. That gave me the right values in life. Other people have a big influence over how you're brought up and how you're disciplined, but once you get old enough to know about the Lord and have faith in Him, it makes a big difference in how you live and look at the world. He's the One who created everything, the One who controls the world and what goes on. You can't influence that; you simply have to have faith in Him. The toughest thing about losing John was that he wasn't just my brother--he was my best friend. He was easy going and he loved to have fun. No matter what you were doing, if John was around, everybody was laughing. It's hard to lose someone like that. He was the youngest boy in our family, seven years younger than me. I was already racing before he got out of grade school. When I moved to North Carolina back in '90, he came along to work for me. He, another guy and myself were building the cars, hanging the bodies--doing all the stuff. Then when he left Florida Southern College, he started racing, too. At first, John knew nothing about racing. So the other guys on the team and I taught him the right way to do it. He was very successful in racing because of that.

Back when he first started, he would amaze me with the things he could do. He would start in the back and pass other cars on the outside. No one else could ever do that. He'd win every week. The other drivers would get mad at him and wreck him on purpose.

They were all teaming up against him but, somehow, the majority of the time, he'd make it through.

When John passed away, faith in the Lord brought our family through his death. It drew us closer together and made us stronger. And my wife, Andrea, was awesome. She was one of the strongest people there as far as dealing with what was going on with John. When he died, I asked, "Lord, why did this happen to him and not to me? I've been in worse wrecks than that." But I know the Lord works in mysterious ways, so I just pray to Him for support and ask Him to watch over my family and me. Two months after John's death, I won an uncontested Busch series race at Charlotte Motor Speedway and dedicated the race to him. We needed something good to happen to our team and I think John was right there watching out for us. A month later, in June of '97, I named my new baby boy in John's honor, and I took the outside front-row position for the Miller 400 at Michigan. A week later, in California, I won the first pole position of my Winston Cup career. It was neat and amazing. For me, it was proof that God really does listen, but I still don't understand how so many good things could come on the heels of my family's worst tragedy.

I've never really looked way out into the future because I've always concentrated on what I was doing at the time. I still think about John all the time. And because I never know if today will be my last, I try every day to be the best person I can be.

Joe Nemechek and Ron Camacho

The Power of Family

Some of the nation's oldest racetracks are in the Northeast. I think there are more racetracks in New York State and Pennsylvania than in any other state in the country.

There are traditions in racing in the Northeast that most of the country doesn't even understand. Indianapolis may go back to the early 1900's, but look at Thompson Speedway in Connecticut. Even with the popularity of motor sports now in this country, people tend to think that because of Winston Cup's popularity, the sport was born in the South. I think you'll find that the sport was born as a profession in the Northeast.

The success of my families racing legacy goes all the way back to my grandfather, Eli. I never really got a chance to know him. He passed away when I was very young. He was very outspoken and, by trade, a very successful chicken and dairy farmer on the Pennsylvania border of upstate New York.

Back in the 40's, he and my grandmother spent their summers at a house they owned in Florida. That's when the beach races at Daytona were just getting started. My grandfather became a huge racing fan, first following the beach races in Florida and then going to some of the local dirt tracks in New York State.

In 1949, after summering in Florida, he returned to New York with the idea of building a racetrack. He carved out a little 1/4-mile dirt track near his dairy farm. The track opened for business with races scheduled every Saturday night. We might just be farmers today in upstate New York if not for the success of my grandfather's and my father's passion

94

for the sport of racing. He continued to farm and operate the racetrack until his health failed.

My father was named Eli, just like my grandfather. He had a heart of gold and would help anybody he could. Besides owning a racetrack, dad also ran a dairy store and a bakery. I guess you could say his plate was always full. My dad was one of the real pioneers of motor sports in New York State. He saw motor sports as a viable business and was very involved in trying to organize racing to make it more professional. He even had visions of building a larger racetrack when the Chemung economy wasn't doing well in the mid '70's. It could have worked if they had allowed my dad to build a more modern racing facility there, but the townspeople wouldn't give him permits to build a more modern facility.

It was my dad who decided to quit farming and concentrate on motor sports. After a fire on the dairy farm, he enlarged the track to three-eighths of a mile and it went from dirt to blacktop. Dad operated that racetrack for 25 years. It was a great business. Dad's brothers ran a repair garage and body shop in the town of Chemung, New York. They were involved more on the competitive side of racing.

My brother, Geoff, got his start in racing when he was a teenager, hanging around the repair shop and helping with the cars. As he progressed in his career, I worked on his cars and went to the races with him. Soon, I was involved on the competitive side. I owe a lot to Geoff for allowing me that. Let's face it, when he was 20, I was 10, and who wants their little brother hanging around with them? But he let me travel around the Northeast with him where he literally had to sneak me into the garages because I wasn't old enough to be around the cars.

When I was about 16 years old, my parents wanted me to operate my grandfather's racetrack. I had to make a decision about whether I wanted to continue on with the family racetrack business or pursue a career in racing. I told my parents I wanted to be a racecar driver.

Mom and Dad really didn't want me involved with racing. I was a fairly good golfer in high school and they wanted me to focus on that. Geoff was already getting his racing career established and they felt like one racecar driver in the family was enough. By that time though, I was too involved and I knew racing was my love.

I am very proud to say I drove for Junior Johnson. Back in 1988-89, I drove for Bud Moore and before that, I drove for Hoss Ellington. My big break came in the spring of '87 during the Late Model Sportsman Division. Terry Labonte was driving for Junior Johnson and was injured in a crash at Darlington. There were two short tracks in North Wilkesboro and Bristol. Junior and the powerhouse Budweiser team asked me to relief drive for Labonte. I finished eighth and ninth, had two top-ten finishes and got noticed by other Winston Cup car owners. I drove about 18 races for Hoss Ellington's Bulls-Eye Bar-B-Q team, but driving for Junior was probably the biggest endorsement I could have ever gotten.

My younger brother, Todd, also got into racing. Even though it's our job to be competitive on the racetrack, Todd, Geoff and I never competed off the track in anything. We have a responsibility to our sponsors and to our race teams. We compete as hard as we can against whoever it is out there. But off the track, we're just family.

I'm glad that my family runs my team. My wife, Diane, and I had some real tough times back in 1997. We bought the team in 1995 from Junior Johnson and barely made it through when a sponsorship didn't pay. We couldn't compete at 100% in those days because I was trying to drive very cautiously on the racetrack. We couldn't afford to tear up the equipment. At one point, we had to put the payroll on our personal credit cards to keep business going. We didn't have enough money to do what we were doing, but Diane and my sister-in-law, Donna, just made it happen.

Then, we took on a partner who decided to come in and steal the race team away from us. Finally, through a great sponsorship in '98 and '99 from Paychex, a company out of Rochester, New York, we were able to buy back 100% ownership of the race team and now we've got things going in the right direction. It's been a tremendous struggle for the last three to four years, but we're determined to make this work.

I believe you should never underestimate the power of a family business and the strength that comes from everyone pulling in the same direction and working toward a common goal. Our business is very demanding and competitive on and off the track. Who can you depend on more than your family? My wife, sister-in-law, father-in-law and various cousins work for our team.

Even my daughter, Heidi, who is 22, helps with the fan mail and my appearance schedule. When she was young, it was very difficult to have the family with me. Kids weren't allowed in the pit and we didn't have a place to keep a motor home. I missed a lot of Heidi's growing up years. But, you're going to run across hardships and bumps in the road. There may be disagreements and disappointments, but the love of a family should always come through and win in the end. That's the success of your business no matter what your business is.

There's no question that my family has done everything to keep this race team going. We're a very good support group for each other through the hard times. Our community of NASCAR Winston Cup drivers, car owners, mechanics--even the Public Relations people--is one big family. If someone needs help or is having a hard time, we're there for support. The wives, especially, are the backbone, and the dedication and hard work of the MRO (Motor Racing Outreach) has pulled that family spirit together at the racetrack. NASCAR has allowed us to bring our motor homes and given us a place to be a community of neighbors. We are a family on and off the track.

I remember an incident in '92 when Kyle Petty's car crashed and caught fire at Martinsville. My brother, Geoff, was the first one on the scene with former Navy seal and pit boss, Tony Liberati. With Geoff's background as a volunteer fireman back in Chemung, it didn't surprise me a bit that he was the first one there with a fire extinguisher. He wasn't afraid. He felt compelled to go into the flames that were engulfing Petty's car. Liberati helped free Petty from his helmet, which had been strapped to his shoulder harness to prevent whiplash. Geoff putting out that fire was an unselfish act of courage and sacrifice.

When Geoff had that devastating crash in Daytona, our family's support was everything. I was standing on top of my motor home in the competitor compound at Daytona Speedway when he crashed. From where I stood, it was out of my viewing so I didn't know the extent of it. I got down and went into the mobile home where my father-in-law was watching it all on TV. He was white as a ghost when he said, "It's really bad." I took off for the infield care center, but when I got there, they didn't know if he was even alive.

Up to that point, I hadn't seen a replay of the wreck, but at the center, a closed circuit TV showed the wreckage and there wasn't much left of the vehicle. I could hear the two-way radios of the safety people. Finally, I saw Geoff reach up and move his oxygen mask. That was my first sign that he was alive. They took him directly to Halifax Hospital instead of the care center, so I knew he must have had some pretty serious injuries.

I was certainly tense all the way to the infield care center, and I prayed. One of the first people I saw when I got to Halifax was Michael Waltrip. He was very concerned. That just goes to show you what our sport is about caring for each other.

Through all the trials and tribulations, your faith has to be very, very strong or this sport will eat you up. There are more disappointments than there are rewards. Sometimes you wonder, "Am I capable of doing a good job? Can I keep doing this?" Then, you have to take a step back and realize that there are only 50 of us in the world who do this. That's a pretty small and elite group. The bottom line is that we have all been past champions from some place in the country. You have to take pride in that. There are 42 losers and one winner every weekend. It's not about learning how to become a good loser, you just have to learn to truly analyze the situation and take the good with the bad. It's about being realistic and being happy in your environment and the idea that you have to constantly improve and keep that burning desire to win.

It's not just about shooting corks in a winner's circle of confetti. Sometimes, race fans will say, "Well, he's too old. He's had an accident. He's gotten soft. He's not competitive anymore." I don't know of any driver who goes on that track who doesn't want to win that race. They may be very realistic about their chances, but every one of them is competitive and wants to win. Being in the winners' circle is a very big part, visually, but it's a very small part of the heart and soul of racing.

During troubled times, the world is so full of hurdles and sometimes we do other things for strength that are the wrong things. Ultimately, you need the support of your family and to seek the Lord's help and invite Him to be your ultimate guide and strength.

Brett Bodine

CHAPTER FOUR
The Race

"No matter how good you're running, or how bad you're running, finish the race."
Alan Kulwicki

Booing Is Good

When I first started winning races, I didn't understand where all the booing came from. I thought I must have done something wrong or offended someone. Maybe I said something I shouldn't have said. It really affected me. I was especially bothered for people who were close to me, like Brooke and my parents or my fans. I know that it bothered them a lot at first and I was trying to understand it and get to the bottom of it. Why were they booing me?

The more I researched the booing, the more I understood that it is not so much a negative thing. It showed the loyalty of the fans to our sport, not necessarily for me, but they were pulling for their driver. They wanted to see multiple winners and they were pulling for the underdog. When there is one guy out there dominating all the time and winning a lot of races, they want to see him get beaten. That's the way these people express their feelings. I took it all personally when it first happened. Then I prayed about it and I think that God helped me understand that it wasn't about anything that I did, other than doing something right. I was doing everything I could do to be honest and do my best on the racetrack. The booing almost became a reward.

I had first noticed the booing when I was bound for the championship in '95. I would say that a lot of it stemmed from fans of Earnhardt, or maybe even Rusty Wallace. We were the guys battling for the race wins and the championship, especially Earnhardt. There became a rivalry, not necessarily between Earnhardt and myself. We are competitors and we

102

want to finish ahead of one another, but we respected each other and what was left on the track was on the track. What was off the track was separate, but a rivalry seemed to develop between our fans.

The only occasion that it really hurt me was when I crashed. I was inside the car and couldn't really hear much, but Brooke and my crew chief, Ray, would tell me that people cheered when I crashed. That bothered me because that goes further than just a friendly rivalry to me. When somebody's life is on the line and people are cheering, you do take it personally.

Then I remembered how Dale Earnhardt himself had helped prepare me for this. In '93 I would hear people cheering for him when I rode around the track with him during drive introduction. A couple of times I would see flags with the number three on them and right next to them see a three with a circle and a cross through it. Right then Dale said, "As long as they're making noise, you are going to be happy because you're doing something right." When I was racing for the championship and the "boos" outweighed the cheers, I thought, "This has got to be good."

I had really been hardened for a couple of years while racing to get ahead. I had been so focused on winning the championship that I had really tried to put all my feelings behind me. At a sports banquet in '95, I broke down and cried. My dad said, "The old Jeff is back." As you attend awards banquets and get trophies or cries from the audience along the way after winning the championship or a big race, it emotionally takes you over. I was overwhelmed and all of us had this feeling of disbelief. I had accomplished this ultimate goal I had only dreamed of and I guess that was the way that I expressed it.

It is easy to get a big head and feel that you did all this yourself. But then you realize that you are not the one in control and you are not the one that's doing it. God is really in control. We lose more races than we win. The only way you can really be content with finishing second is to have God in your life because it gives you peace of mind. When you win, it allows you to give the praise and recognition to Him. When you don't win, it allows you to just say, "Hey, this is a part of racing and a part of life." Every year I have grown to be more humble and appreciate everything in my life and to understand that not every finish on the track or everything that happens on the weekend is my whole life. It is not who I am, it is just what I do.

Brooke has had a huge influence in my life. I'm not saying I was heading in a bad direction, but she helped me to keep my priorities straight. I still sin and make mistakes, but I feel like Brooke's moral values have helped me to keep God in my life and to remember what is important.

For me, this sport is not really about being the best racecar driver out there. I know that there are a lot of people out there that think that I have accomplished what I wanted. But this is about more than a championship and statistics to me. This is about how I've impacted the sport and the people that follow it.

What makes me the happiest is when fans and other people I'm around come up to me and say, "We appreciate your Christian witness and the role model you are for our children." That means far more to me than going out there and winning races.

Jeff Gordon, Max Helton and Ron Camacho

The Race

Tony Stewart's Three Wheeler

"It is a wise father that knows his own child."
Shakespeare

People always say to me, "You're Tony's dad, you could be on the rig or in the pits. Why do you sit in the stands when you're at his races?" I sit in the stands because I just flat-out love to watch my son race. Tony is such a magnificent racer that you just can't fully appreciate what he does from the pits because you can't see the whole track.

When I can be at the track, I sit in the stands and just watch him race. When I'm not at the track, he calls me when he gets home to talk about the race. It might be late...but he calls. He called at 2:45 in the morning when he finally got back to Charlotte after winning his first race at Richmond. I expected his call. I went to bed and Tony called me, like he always does. His first words started with, "What are you doing?"

"What do you think I'm doing," I said. "It's 2:45 a.m., I'm sleeping." I kid him about it but I always look forward to his calls after a race, no matter what time they come in and no matter how he does.

When did I first know he had this talent? That's easy. When he was a young kid on his three-wheeler, he'd spend hour after hour, on his own, learning to perfectly balance himself up on two wheels in either direction.

Nelson Stewart and Claire B. Lang

"I'm Alive!"

I grew up racing motorcycles in Southern California. I got so beat up that my parents wouldn't let me race bikes anymore. My mom couldn't stand watching me race as a kid because she was afraid I would get hurt. My dad loved racing, he loved the battle. But, if I fell, that's where he had the problem. My dad could not stand being in the hospital or being wherever I was if I was injured. That's where my mom would step in. I had reconstructive knee surgery when I was 8 years old and they had to totally rebuild my knee. When they popped the x-rays on the machine in front of the light, my dad passed out. They brought in another stretcher to put him on.

My parents were both watching the crash that afternoon of June 25, 2000. It was the Busch Series race at Watkins Glen and we had an awesome day going. I was really looking forward to the road course race and we were sticking to our plan on fuel strategy. We came out of the pits and had completed only one lap when it happened.

The brakes failed. I was looking underneath the lapped car and I got on the brake pedal and the brake pedal went to the floor. I knew I only had one move-- and I thought about running into the back of the car in front of me, but I was going so fast. I thought, "Man, I'm not going to hurt him, as well." So, I turned to the right trying to get into the inside wall, but as soon as I got into the infield grass, the car went straight again and bounced around and left the racetrack.

I was airborne and cleared the sand trap. In the air, I thought, "Man this is really going to be bad." I was expecting it to be concrete and, when I was in the air, I just lowered my head down to my chest, so I wouldn't get whiplash. I pulled my feet back and relaxed my body as much as I could so I would be limber when I hit.

I saw a deal on television that I'm sure everybody has seen with Rusty Wallace, Kenny Schrader, a whole bunch of different guys talking about their big crashes. Every one of them talks about how they lowered their head and relaxed themselves for the crash.

I don't know what inside of me remembered that show when I was doing 140 miles per hour about ready to crash. One thing that worked for me is that I knew there was nothing I could do. I was in trouble and there was this calming attitude. It was like, "OK, here it comes and it's going to be big...be ready." I just tried to stay relaxed, closed my eyes and put my life in the Lord's hands. I knew my parents, my family, my girlfriend and friends were watching and I really thought they'd be taking me out of there unconscious.

Then, I hit the wall. The car was on fire and I was sitting in a pile of thermal foam thinking, "Oh man, my legs are okay, my body is alright, my arms work."

I put my window net down and the fans went crazy. When I got out of the car they were jumping up and down with their arms in the air and this adrenaline rush came over me.

Next thing you know, I was on the roof of the car. I had my arms up in the air just thankful that God was riding with me on that one. It was like a victory salute on top of the car and I was thinking, "I'm alive!"

Jimmie Johnson and Claire B. Lang

The Day Rusty Wallace Made History

Rumor has it
History was made this day,
As a NASCAR Champion
Passed our way.
He said he had the fastest car on the street
"There's nothing on wheels I can't beat."
This astronaut
By the name of John Glenn
Said, "Come over closer
I'd like to speak with you friend.
I've got this leftover trinket
I knew NASA would never miss,
And I've been waiting
For a special occasion, just like this.
It, too has wheels
But I don't use them much.
They're just a drag on my boosters
When I pop the clutch.
So if you think you're bragging
Is actual fact,
I challenge you to race

The Race

On the Bonneville Salt Flats."
Without exaggeration,
It happened this way
I know
'Cause I got it from a friend
Who got it from a friend
This very day.
Everyone knew
It was going to be tough
But our boy John Glenn
He had the right stuff.
Well, if we only knew
How wrong we could be
When we all gathered
At the finish line to see.
Both vehicles were coming
In a cloud of dust,
Wallace was the name
The crowd shouted at us.
Then I heard one man loudly muddle...
"GOOD GOD, ALMIGHTY!
RUSTY WALLACE JUST PASSED
THE AMERICAN SPACE SHUTTLE!"
John Glenn's face
Was turning three shades of green.
When he saw he had been beaten
By the Wallace machine.
But to Rusty Wallace
He just yawwwnnned with a sigh
Cause he knew he'd been born
With a license to fly.

By Randy J. Poyer - ©1992

Chocolate

What scares me the most in racing is not the danger, but the fear of letting down my teammates. Even though I've been the gasman on a Winston Cup crew for nearly 20 years, working week in and week out with a seven-time Winston Cup champion, I still worry about letting down the team. It's tracks like Daytona or Talladega where I know that the tires are gonna' run a whole lot longer than that tank of gas; where it comes down to a gas-and-go and I'm the only one out there. Now, that's scary.

One of the most frightening moments of my career came this past season at the Daytona 500. While making a routine pit stop, I turned with my second can of fuel and a tire from another car behind us rolled under my feet and tripped me. I almost panicked, but I knew I had to get that car full of gas. Even though I was nearly on the ground with a 90-pound gas can hoisted up above me, I still managed to get the car full of gas.

Racing is an adrenaline rush—not just for the race fans, but even for us old crewmembers that have literally grown up in this sport. When the car comes roaring down pit road, I get really pumped up. I'm standing there waiting with my foot up on the wall. The gas can sitting on my left shoulder is, oddly enough, light as a feather during the heat of battle, but weighs a ton after the race, that is how focused I am. I don't even look at the car; I'm looking at the other members of my team because I key off of them. In the back of my head I'm running through this whole process of pitting the car—something I've done a thousand times before. When the car stops, I step over the wall and I don't see another thing that goes on around me. I don't see the car that has whirled in a foot away from my leg. I don't see the other cars running down pit road beside me at incredible speeds. The only thing I see is that hole where I am to plug the gas can in and make sure the tank is full.

About the only other thing I am aware of during a 15-second pit stop is the other members of my team. A good pit crew has to work well together. You have to be aware of what each one is doing, because even though there are seven of us over the wall, we are one unit. We win together and we lose together. Not one member of our team is more important than the other. The person who washes the windshield or the person who gives Dale Earnhardt a drink of water is just as important as the person putting in the fuel or jacking up the car.

You know, I've been around racing all my life. My dad was Bobby Myers, one of the early pioneers in NASCAR racing. He died in the 1957 Southern 500 while driving for Lee Petty. My uncle was Billy Myers, a former Grand National champion. I was only 9 years old when my dad died, so I grew up without a dad. I think about that a lot—what it might have been like to grow up with a dad.

The day my daddy died we moved to my grandmother's house. She made us go to church every time the church bells rang. What made it so bad was that the church was right next-door. I went to church until I was too big for Grandma to make me go. I started hanging out with the wrong crowd, trying about everything there was to try. I was "cool," but I still wasn't happy. I thought for a while that I would try to follow in my dad's footsteps and drive racecars, but

I soon ran out of money and needed a way to support myself. After hopping from job to job, I decided that I wanted to work on race cars. An old buddy from my youth, Richard Childress, had just started a race team. I went in and asked Richard for a job and a few minutes later, I was working. That was 1983.

When I first got on the road and starting traveling to a different city every weekend, it was one big party. I mean, I could tell you what the inside of every bar in Daytona Beach looked like, but I couldn't tell you where one single church in the whole town was.

I was one of the wild bunch. I'd race hard during the day, and party even harder at night. It seemed like I had everything a man could ever want, but my life was empty. It was completely dead.

Max Helton, a new chaplain in racing, came onto the scene. Max and all his Christian buddies would hold "prayer meetings" in the middle of the garage before the race, while we dedicated crewmembers were busy trying to get the car on the line. I was really put out with these people. They were just so—happy. Max would invite me to come to the meetings, but I was always too busy. Even if I had nothing to do, I'd make up a reason not to go. Not to mention, there was that aggravating Darrell Waltrip who was going to that thing, and that's all I wanted to hear was Darrell talking some more. No wonder they called him "Jaws."

About this same time, I met Caron, a young, dark-haired, sports journalist in Florida. I asked her out to a party and she accepted. I could tell there was something different about her. The next night we went out again and I was the perfect gentleman. But on night number three, she told me that we could be friends, but that's all. She told me that if that's the way

I lived my life that was fine, but it wasn't the way she lived hers. She went on and told me that Jesus Christ was the only person who was ever going to change my life, and that He was the only road to happiness.

The next day I apologized to Caron for my behavior and promised her that I would never, ever have another drink. I've kept that promise. Caron has been my wife now for seven years.

Since I've accepted Jesus Christ in my life, there have been things that I wish I could go back in time and fix. I know that my pickin' and playin' have hurt a lot of feelings. I'd love to be able to go back and tell the folks that I hurt along the way in my life how sorry I am. Today I go around talking to kids at schools and telling them the story of how Jesus Christ has made such a difference in my life--even in public schools! I tell them that, even though I grew up without a father, I have a Heavenly Father who loves me, even when I'm unlovable to anybody else.

When we were in Atlanta for the final race, two years ago, Max stood up in the service and asked if anyone would like to stand up and say what MRO has meant to them. Darrell Waltrip stood and said, "You know, a lot of people used to not like me. I ran my mouth a lot and said a lot of things I shouldn't have said and through MRO, it has really changed my life and I just want to say 'thanks' to MRO."

Darrell sat down and Max asked, "Who's next?"

I stood up and said, "Yeah, well I am one of the guys who didn't like Darrell because he ran his mouth so much. But because of MRO, I love him in the Lord. Hey, man, he's my brother!"

Chocolate and Caron Meyers

113

Thanks to Earnhardt

My racing career began in central California with many successes at local tracks. I became the track champion at Stockton and decided to move to North Carolina to further my career. My dad and some of my friends had already moved there, making the transition better.

After a few years of racing at the Concord Speedway, I was trying to make my way into NASCAR's premier series, Winston Cup. Marc Reno, a friend from California, and I built a racecar and planned to run it at Richmond, Virginia in our first attempt at this level of racing.

Ken Schrader, who had been racing Winston Cup cars for about two years, and I became friends. He would stop by my shop to see Marc and me. Marc and I were working on a car to race in Winston Cup and had planned on entering it at the Richmond race. On some occasions, Kenny would bring his buddy, Dale Earnhardt, to our shop. One day we were sitting and talking and Dale noticed that we were building a racecar and asked, "What are you guys doing with that?" Marc said, "We're going to go up to Richmond to race." Out of the blue, Schrader said, "Earnhardt, you ought to sponsor this car." When they left, Schrader told Marc that he would talk to Earnhardt more about it. We were glad Kenny was going to talk with Dale and get back to us tomorrow.

The next day, Kenny came to our shop with the deal. "Earnhardt is going to sponsor your car." Man, were we excited! I responded, "How much money is he going to give us?" Schrader said, "He's not giving you any money." Marc said, "You have to give us some money." Kenny said, "No, he will give you credibility." Earnhardt is one of the most popular and successful racers in NASCAR. We didn't have any other offers so we decided to take his offer, realizing that we would draw a lot of attention with DALE EARNHARDT's name on the car. That hadn't been done before. Dale had just started a Chevrolet dealership in Newton, North Carolina, so he had us paint "DALE EARNHARDT CHEVROLET" on the side of our car.

This was all exciting for me. All the best drivers (my heroes) were there; Richard Petty, Darrell Waltrip, Dale Earnhardt, Rusty Wallace and others. This was a dream come true. I qualified twentieth but had problems early in the race.

Earnhardt decided that he would sponsor my car again at Charlotte--this time with $3,000 for the paint job that he wanted to put on the car. I went to Charlotte and qualified for the race. Before the race began, Earnhardt came over to give some advice, "You need to stay out of trouble and run this whole race. If I drive by and you've crashed, I will stop my car, get out and whoop your butt." I said, "Okay." This was Dale Earnhardt, a champion racer, talking to me--a rookie. I wasn't about to argue with him.

As the race got underway, I was running as hard as I could but trying to stay out of trouble. I was running about twentieth and Earnhardt was leading the race. Suddenly, a wreck was up in front of me. As I went by I saw it was Earnhardt. He was sitting down on the apron of the track. I thought maybe I should stop and get out and whoop his butt. I was feeling cocky because I knew that I had finished better than him.

A few years later, after several rides in different racecars, I started driving the Kodak car of Larry McClure's. I had a couple of wins with him in 1990. In February of each year the great stock car classic, the Daytona 500, is run. During practice, leading up to the 500, I was fast. But no one was paying much attention to it since Dale Earnhardt and Davey Allison were the favorites to win. Dale had never won the 500 and now he was on a mission.

As I started the race, I was really fast and was able to run near the front all day. Near the end, I was leading the race when Earnhardt passed me with twelve laps to go for the lead. Then a caution came out. The race was restarted with ten laps to go. Earnhardt was leading with me right behind him. He out jumped me on the restart and pulled away about ten car lengths. I thought my chances for a win were about over. Davey Allison comes flying up behind me and we started drafting up to Earnhardt. With three laps to go I was able to get a run at Earnhardt coming out of the fourth turn. I took the lead through the tri-oval and pulled away from Earnhardt as I looked in my mirror to see him and Davey racing side by side, headed onto the backstretch. Then suddenly, Earnhardt and Allison crashed into each other bringing out a caution flag with only two laps to go. As I came back to the finish fine, I realized that with just two laps to go that the race would end under caution, meaning that I had won the Daytona 500.

Following the pace car by the two wrecked cars, I saw a wrecked Dale Earnhardt and realized that I had passed the man who gave me my break in Winston Cup racing to win a race that he had tried years to win and had failed. I reveled in those moments as I drove to the cheering crowds on the front stretch and saw my team jumping with joy. I was just starting my career in Winston Cup and just passed one of the much-heralded drivers (the same person who gave me creditability but no money to get my start) to win the prestigious Daytona 500.

Ernie Irvan and Max Helton

110% And On Time

I guess I am different than most race drivers because of how late I became involved in racing. My parents, Billy and Mary Lou, had a farm when I was a kid and I had go-carts, motorcycles, played high school football, boxed a little and skied a lot. But I never raced until early 1990 when a friend of mine started racing in motor-cross. I was 20 years old when I told my dad I wanted to motor-cross race and he told me, "No, if you're gonna race, you ought to get into something that'll protect you--like a stockcar."

My dad raced back in the '60's, but he quit in '68 when my mom became pregnant with my sister, Laytona. He didn't think he could make a living at racing, even though it was something he really loved. He liked doing other things, like running his cable TV business; but racing was his one true passion. He didn't try to push me into racing but he did inspire my competitive instinct for it.

I've always loved animals, so when college rolled around, I thought about becoming a veterinarian. But when I found out I had to go to school for eight years, I said, "Forget it! I don't like school that much!" I decided to go into business with my dad's cable company and ended up with a degree in Business Management from the University of Georgia. I'm glad I finished college. My dad made it clear that if I didn't maintain a "B" average there would be no more racing, so I had to work hard. But then, the defining moment for me came the first time I got into a racecar at Lanier Raceway. I knew that's what I wanted to do for a living.

The Race

I raced about six times on the local asphalt track at Lanier. During my fourth race, I was involved in an accident where my car jumped over the guardrail of the track. It scared my mom to death! When the car ran off the track, all she could see was the bottom of the car. By the time she got to me, they had pulled me out from under the car and she didn't know what to think. She said, "You're done racing." Once she calmed down, I showed her that all the damage was to the sheet metal and that the sheet metal is not what protects you; it's the roll cage. When she saw that, she felt better. She wears a radio now when she's at a race. If something happens, she'll know immediately what's going on. We know that racing can be dangerous, but we don't talk about it. I think she liked it better when I played football.

I drive back to our farm in Georgia every chance I get because that's where my mom is. She's always been there for me. Whenever we're together, we joke around and laugh and always have a good time. She's been more than just my mom; she's been my friend.

Dad always told me that whatever I do--whether it's playing football, baseball or basketball--always put in one hundred and ten percent or don't do it at all; and always be on time. He said he wouldn't stand for anything less. You might call that pushing, but it was good. He taught me a lot about life and has helped and guided me since day one. I learned more from my dad than I ever learned in college. He is probably my biggest critic, but he's also my biggest fan.

You can't trust what a lot of people say these days, but you can trust my dad. He lives by his word. Nobody who ever met him has ever had anything bad to say about him. If he says he's going to do something, then you know he's going to do it. That's one of the things I admire most about him. Nothing compares to my relationship with my dad. We're the best of friends. We also have many of the same views when it comes to the business operations of the race team. We talk all the time and he takes care of the business with sponsors.

I take my relationship with my sponsors very seriously. Keebler and Brunswick have invested a lot and made a great commitment to me and I am committed to them. Through our business relationships we have managed to become friends over the years.

If I had to pick one driver I really admire, I'd have to say it is Mark Martin. I like his driving style and pretty much everything about him. Sometimes he'll just lay back and then he'll come to the front. He never pushes the car at the beginning of the race. If someone is faster than him, he'll just pull over and let them go.

When you're on the track, you think about racing someone the way you want them to race you. You think about doing your very best week in and week out and always strive to do better. One of the hardest times for me was in the beginning of my racing career in 1995. It was tough making some of the first races. We worked so hard, just like all the teams out there and there's no worse feeling than being one of those teams that doesn't make the race and being sent home. But then, the best feeling in the world for me was winning my first race--the Sears Auto Center 250 in Milwaukee in July 1996. It took me awhile to realize what happened. Another really great moment was getting the 1998 NASCAR Busch Series Most Popular

Driver Award. It meant so much to me to be recognized by the racing fans. After every race, no matter how well I do, I try to spend time at the souvenir trailer signing autographs and talking to fans. I really love the fans, especially the kids. I don't have any of my own yet but they're definitely in the picture.

The great thing about NASCAR is that it's one big family and everyone makes you feel welcome. The most important thing to me is family, mom and dad, my brother, Glen, my sister, Laytona, and my wife, Jina. She is so supportive, traveling to every race and always being there for me. We dated in high school and we got married in 1998. Most people graduate from college; move away and they don't see their family a lot. I get to see mine every weekend because they always come to my races. It's great to have a career where I am doing something I love and have my family around me, too.

I get to meet a lot of people in this business. I got a letter the other day from a 13-year old boy. He doesn't play any sports, and he's really short. I know people pick on him all the time. I can relate to that because I'm 29 years old and I'm short. People used to pick on me all the time, too. But racing gave me the desire to be competitive and I want to race as long as I can compete. I know there will be times when I'm not the winner, but when I can't compete anymore, that's when I'll step down. In the meantime, there's really no better job.

Buckshot Jones

A True Racing Fan

There is a certain naiveté in racing. In the beginning, it was built on danger; that's what made racing--daredevil drivers facing death at every turn. There were no roofs, roll cages or roll bars. If the car flipped, chances were 50/50 the driver would be killed. Today's stockcar drivers are insulated from those things; if the car turns over, he might get banged up a little bit. The possibility of death is always there, but the likelihood is low. So greatness has to be related to the danger involved. Many writers have never seen any of the great drivers.

One of the wonderful things about racing is that there's something in it for everyone. Stock car racing is a very narrow stage in the vast theater of American racing. Those who love to work with tools and mechanical things gravitate to drag racing.

During the depression, there were two forms of entertainment that flourished: movies and auto racing. I guess it was because people needed entertainment.

I'm from Ridgewood, in northern New Jersey, a product of the depression. We had no money for anything. My father was a linguist; he spoke nine languages. Every morning, he would do the New York Times crossword puzzle and finish it in short order. He was constantly on my back about words, pronunciation, diction, and elocution.

There was a race track in the next town. I used to hear the cars roaring; it was like a magnet to a kid in short pants. I'd go under, over or around the fence to see those cars until I met a racer who showed me how to lie down on the running board-- opposite the ticket-taker of an incoming car--so I could get in for nothing.

I got into racing through a succession of events. I was aware of a newspaper, *Bergen Herald*, that had a section devoted to auto racing--a broadsheet. One day, as I was walking down the street of my hometown, I looked through the window of this *Ridgewood News* and there it was--lying there on the press, in tabloid form, about to be printed.

That first edition of this newspaper came out in August of 1934. I went in and got some to sell at the track that weekend. It was a way of getting into the racetrack for nothing and making money at the same time. I did that up until World War II. I went into the Army, came back, and resumed my racing interest. I kept taking newspapers to the tracks, but by then, I was getting other people to sell them.

One weekend in 1947, I took papers with me to two different tracks and got a guy to sell them on Friday night. We sold 400 copies. Then on Saturday night, I took some to the next track, about 60 miles away. There was a bigger crowd, but I only sold about 40 copies. I couldn't understand the disparity in the sales. Why would we sell so many in one place and so few in another? Then it dawned on me. The difference was the announcer. On Friday night, the track announcer said, "Hey, see the latest edition of the *National Speed Sport News*, page five--wow!" Everyone is talking about it. On Saturday, the other announcer said, "See the latest issue; it's a quarter. Buy it." Nothing. So I decided that if being an announcer was the way to sell papers, I'd become an announcer. And I did.

My first announcing job was at the Selinsgrove Track in central Pennsylvania in 1948. I was friends with this race driver, Buster Keller, who said, "You know, Chris, my father and I are going to become the promoters at Selinsgrove. You know these cars. If you want to be an announcer, come and be our announcer." I was pretty good at it. In fact, I was so good at it that I was suddenly in demand all over the country. I was the track announcer at Daytona Beach all through the '50's. When they opened the Daytona Speedway in 1959, I was the track announcer there. "Here they come, there they go!"

In 1960, CBS came to Daytona and did a television show on a day of meaningless racing created just for television. They did two races: one on the oval and one on the infield road coarse. Walter Cronkite and Art Peck were the announcers. At the time, Cronkite was an amateur sports car driver in an Austin Healey. The show got very bad reviews.

A year later, in 1961, when ABC launched its Wild World of Sports, the network contacted the Daytona Speedway and said, "We'd like to televise your July 4th Firecracker 250." NASCAR replied, "Go back to New York. You were here last year and you smelled out the place. Thanks, but no thanks." ABC said, "No, no, no...that was CBS. We're ABC." The Daytona view was that these guys were all the same.

ABC persisted. They asked Bill France what his complaint was with the CBS telecast. He told them, "Well, the announcers didn't understand." They said, "Well, we have Jim McKay." France said, "Don't tell me about Jim McKay; they had Walter Cronkite." They kept on bugging him. Finally, they asked him what they could do to get him to change his mind. France replied, "Well, you can get yourself an announcer who knows and understands the sport." They asked, "Where can we find this guy?" He said, "Well, you can use my guy." That's how I got pushed into television.

So in 1961, I went to work for ABC's Wild World of Sports. Roone Arledge, who created the show, said he didn't care how good or bad a sporting event was, he was more concerned with its image. Image is everything. The Indianapolis 500 has this incredible image. It's a beautiful track and not a hard race to drive; it's smooth with safety precautions everywhere. Some little tracks are much harder to drive and achieve on, but they don't have the image. Drivers will tell you that Daytona and Talladega are the two easiest tracks on which to drive a racecar. All you do is sit there and keep your foot down.

So who are the great drivers? They aren't necessarily the ones who win at Indianapolis or Daytona or Talladega. There have been accomplished drivers in stock car racing and some that brought the sport to where it is today.

Fireball Roberts was a showman; it had nothing to do with his ability behind the wheel. He was a good driver, but more importantly, he knew how to fill the role. He knew what to say and how to handle the public. To do well in racing today, you have to be a sponsor's dandy. You have to know what to say, how to kiss the sponsor's wife's hand and what fork to use. In Fireball's day, a driver didn't have to do all that. He just had to say or do something that would get the public's attention.

Richard Petty is called "The King" because of his ability and his way of relating to his public. In Petty's early days, the sport was struggling and there weren't many fans, but he interacted extremely well with them. Those fans would come down to his car after the race and he would sign autographs for hours and hours and hours. As the sport grew, Petty grew with it; he became the central figure, the Pied Piper of the drivers. When some new driver would show up and see Petty sitting on the front fender of his car signing autographs, he understood why Petty was the guy getting all the publicity. Then he'd say, "So that's how it's done," and then he'd sign autographs, and the next one would sign autographs, too. The Petty policy and practice soon became standard for NASCAR drivers.

Jeff Gordon is a superb driver....a driver who has an incredible feel for a car on the track. He also has a very accomplished way of communicating with those around him to make sure his car is what it needs to be to win races.

Dale Earnhardt has a good number of the drivers buffaloed with his intimidating style. Billy Winn was like that. "Get out of my way or I'll run you over." That's part of the show business of racing. Earnhardt would never admit it, but that's what it is.

Although racing is considerably safer today than it was years ago, it's pretty hard not to have an occasional death because, physically, it's a very dangerous sport even though cars are made remarkably safer. In the '30's, it seemed like in every issue of my newspaper it was reported someone got killed somewhere.

Of today's stock car drivers, Tony Stewart is a classic example of a driver with an edge. To him, second place is losing. Now, because of the unfortunate practice of paying drivers to race instead of making them earn their prize money--as was the case for many years--a driver's willingness to drive hard, get out on the track and take chances goes away. Drivers get paid whether they win, lose or draw.

That hasn't yet touched Stewart because he grew up having to excel to be paid; he wasn't paid to drive, he was paid to win.

The man-machine equation is so much different today than in the past. Then, drivers won the races always. Now cars win the races; it doesn't matter who drives. The car has to be right and it has to be balanced. Back in the 20's, right up through the 50's, all cars were dogs. A driver had to manhandle his car to win the race.

From that perspective, the best driver I ever saw was Bob Sweikert. He built his own cars, built his own engines and won races. Sweikert was a dirt-and-asphalt track racer who'd turned left his whole life. He was invited to go down to Sebring for the Twelve Hours of Endurance race, a road race where two drivers shared a car. He rode with a wealthy guy who had a very fine car but was a lousy driver. Sweikert was driving a car he had to shift during the course of the race; it was different from anything he'd ever before driven.

During the race, Sweikert would get the car in the lead, but every time he stopped for gas and got out, his partner would drive and go backwards. Then Sweikert would again work his way back up to the lead, only to surrender it to his teammate who would go backwards again. If Sweikert had had any kind of driving partner, he would have won. I've labeled him one of the greats because he had that ability to adapt to different circumstances.

The advent of technology has changed racing to a degree where the man today is a far less important part of the man-machine equation than he was originally, but I still get very excited being at the races and seeing the men and the machines trying to make time stand still. I've run this newspaper, the *National Speed Sport News*, for 50 years and I've always run it from a fan's perspective. Because I'm still a fan.

Chris Economacki

My Racing Harem

I am the second-generation racer in my family. My father started in 1951, won his first race in 1952, and ran his first NASCAR in 1959 on a road course.

I started racing locally at the Rockford Speedway. Then I moved Into ARTGO, then to ASA, then to USAC's stock car division. In Chicago in the late '70's, you didn't run ARCA or Winston because it was too far away, so the predominant series was USAC. Bobby Allison, A. J. Foyt, and Bobby Unser raced in that, too. Since 1982, I've run ARCA. I've run the truck series and Winston Cup, but I had a wife, two children, and some businesses I didn't want to give up in Chicago, so I just raced the ARCA series. When I had the opportunity nine years ago to sell my three Amoco stations, we moved to Concord, North Carolina. This move was more for my son, Billy, because my career was winding down, but his was just starting.

Being born an Italian in Chicago, of course, you have to be Catholic! Back in Rockford in 1974, I always had a St. Christopher medal on the dash of my car. One day a friend saw it and told me, "You gotta' go with St. Jude because you're hopeless, man! You need the patron saint for the hopeless people!" St. Christopher is the Saint of Travel, but he jumps out at 100 mph, so I wear a St. Jude medallion. Now every race, Billy comes up and takes the chain off me and wears it during the race because he wants to have something of mine with him. It's a tradition.

When Billy first started racing, it was very hard for me to watch him on the track because I was always worried about him. It was very hard to feel he could succeed without my help. But something happened between Billy and me. Now, I not only look at him as my son, but as a competent racecar driver. We talked about the Pettys and the Allisons losing their kids, and that fear is always there, but I now know that this is what Billy really wants to do and I won't take that away from him. For all the years I raced, I didn't have the support of my father.

Billy was born into racing, so by the time he was 11, he understood what was going on. Once he was old enough, he was my spotter then my tire changer. When he was 18 he started to race Legend cars. Then I made the mistake in '94 when I built two new ARCA cars and took them to Louisville, a short track, to test them before the race. I talked ARCA into letting Billy take the second car out for a shakedown. He was quick with it, so I told him I would let him qualify the car. He made the show, so I had to let him race! I was kind of happy the car broke on the first race. It took him about three races before he out-qualified me. I was ticked; it took me many years to learn how to drive a racecar. But Billy had a natural ability; all we had to do was polish the edges.

Racing is a way of life--a very consuming lifestyle. We sleep, eat, and breathe racing; it's all we've done for twenty-seven years. I have two kids who don't do drugs and never got into trouble; I attribute a lot of that to racing. Racing also motivated me to be more successful in my other businesses because I needed to make money to finance it. I wouldn't give it up for anything, but it really is a big roller coaster ride.

You don't need to win every race. Sometimes you can finish tenth and go home satisfied; sometimes you finish second and it stinks. It depends on what you expected and what you've gotten out of your equipment, your crew, and yourself. When we talk about what racing has done and the memories of racing, it isn't the wins we remember or talk about; it's the night we went to 3 C's BBQ in Texas and I had a little too much of 3 C's Red Eye and drove the motor home down the railroad tracks instead of the street, or the night Billy got in a scuffle at the track with Larry Foyt. Those are the memories and stories you cherish. But of all the racing we have done over the years as a family, I will probably best be remembered for my all-girl pit crew. We pioneered the fast pit stops. I won my first ARCA National Championship in 1987 with an all-female pit crew.

My wife, Cathy, and I got the idea for the all-girl pit crew in the early '80's on a trip to Daytona for Speed Week. We were trying to generate better publicity for me. When we got back to Chicago, I took out an ad in *Speed Sports News* that read, "No pay, lousy hours, lots of fun." We didn't get any response, so I put together a crew that included my wife, sisters-in-law, and friends and called them "Bill's Babes." We practiced and practiced working around the Chicago area, but after about a year, it became too expensive so we dismantled the crew.

In 1985, *Sports Illustrated* heard about the pit crew and wanted us to do a reunion. But I didn't want to do a one-time deal; I wanted to do it right. So I called Permatex, the series sponsor of ARCA, and they agreed to sponsor the crew. We had to have special lighter weight equipment designed, and had to practice a lot. The girls were set to debut at Pocono in June, but I hit the wall going into turn one, crashed and got knocked out. I was hospitalized for a few days with amnesia, although I still could remember bits and pieces. When I came to, Cathy was at my bedside when the nurse told me I had been in a crash at Pocono and that I had an all female pit crew. "An all girl pit crew?" I said, "Wow! I've got a freaking harem? Cathy got a little irate and said, "Yeah, you've got a freaking harem and a wife, too!"

Bill Venturini and Ron Camacho

My Heart of Racing

Racing...you either hate it or you love it. You spend your $15 and sit in the grandstands or your $20-$25 and go into the pits. But when you love it, you go every weekend, rain or shine. If it does rain, you do the meanest rain dance known to the stockcar race fan.

Racing, like some other sports, seems to be handed down generation to generation. If your grandfather raced and your dad raced, the odds are you will race. Every now and then, the tradition falls into the female hands of the family and this can be good also, as women are the up and coming stars of our great sport.

When you really think about the words, "heart of racing," you have to consider the days when races were run on wooded boards and sandy beaches. Racers would drive their cars to the track and, hopefully, be able to drive them home. Otherwise they would be in for a long night and a lot of "I told you not to race, dear. Now what are we going to do for a car?" We could say that the heart of racing is the moon shiners and all those moonlight runs they made with bootleg whiskey. No matter what, "The booze must get through." So, they souped up their engines, lightened their cars, and ran like blazes to the nearest safe harbor for a moonshine runner.

Today, this has left us with one true heart and many arteries to racing. The small local tracks may be your heart. They are where it all started and where any and all racers must begin. Jeff Gordon, Bobby and Terry LaBonte, Lee Petty, Richard Petty, Adam Petty, Justin LaBonte, all have that one thing in common.

They all started on small local tracks in Dwarf cars, Mini-stocks, or Street Stocks, but not Winston Cup cars. No one is born with a Winston Cup steering wheel already hooked to the fingers. Some will argue until the sun goes down on what "real" racing is. Is it those 2 1/2 mile super speedways, or the little 1/3 dirt and asphalt tracks that the majority of racers come from or stay at? It is there, at that little track out in the country somewhere that the heart of racing truly comes from. It is not Daytona, Indianapolis, or Las Vegas, but your backyard.

Every Friday night I sit on the top level of my local track and watch the cars hot lap in the sinking golden sun of Florida. The asphalt glows as though it has thousands of diamonds in it. The cars speed by in the purple, pink glow of the setting evening sun, as the full moon rises in a breathtaking display. This is the heart of racing. As the last of the day's sun slowly leaves the track in the still of the evening moon, I know that this is my heart of racing. Here on the small, no banked asphalt and dirt tracks that surround me, I am happy and content and I know that my heart will always remain in the little tracks of yesteryear where everything started.

Jane Smith

That's Racin'!

On a hot Saturday night in August 1977, at the old 1/4 mile dirt track in Concord, North Carolina, the excitement started early--and off the track. A spectator sent his car sailing into a deep, wooded ravine off the backstretch, right before the infield crossover. The woods were so dense that they just left the car in the ditch with all the others that had crashed during the years of racing at the Concord track.

The first heat was pretty exciting. Ralph Earnhardt missed a win because another driver, who was trying to pass him, actually pushed him across the finish line into a second place position. The second heat was not too exciting, but the main event is something I'll never forget. The excitement of it is what brought me back to that little track weekend after weekend. The earlier tension between Ralph Earnhardt and the other driver began again in the final heat. The other driver kept trying to push Earnhardt out of his way again. This time, Earnhardt dropped back, letting most of the traffic pass him. Then, he dove to the inside, pedal to the medal, never letting off. He broadsided the guy who had bumped him during the heat race. It destroyed Earnhardt's car, but the guy who had hit him went sailing over the fourth turn fence and landed upside down. Even though Earnhardt's car was not running, they pointed the black flag at him, disqualifying his earlier second place finish. The fans roared, bought more beer, and cheered Earnhardt as he walked to the infield waving in acknowledgement. Now that's racin'!

Tom Mason

CHAPTER FIVE
The Long Road

*"Victory at all cost, victory in spite of all terror,
victory however long and hard the road may be;
for without victory there is no survival."*
Sir Winston Churchill

I Have Dreams

I never thought too much about what I was going to be when I grew up. If I ever thought about being a grown-up, it was just being a man--a man like my dad. I never really thought about an occupation. I didn't know I could be a racecar driver.

I had many different interests before I raced. There was a time when I was into tropical fish and into ceramics. I made all kinds of ceramic stuff and pottery. Those were the two things I was really interested in before I got going on the racing.

I also loved riding motorcycles. In fact, I wanted to race them, but my dad persuaded me to do stock cars because they're safer. Losing my dad was hard by itself, but made even harder because his death was so tragic. It was way tougher than an illness because with an illness, you're prepared for it. But it's miserable no matter what.

It just left a huge empty hole. You know, the hole fills up in a way, but it sure is slow, and it never fills completely. There will always be a hole there, but now it's not quite as dark and deep. Dad's death brought me closer to my mom, my son Matt, and to my sister, especially with her son's tragedy as well.

I do the best I can at being a father. My son, Matt, is one of the greatest joys in my life. Interacting with him is incredible, and definitely more important than anything else I have ever done. It's also more rewarding. It's a struggle to be a good enough father, which is my nature; I don't feel good enough most of the time, so I do the best I can.

I was 15 when I started racing and 22 when I first

got into NASCAR. I was racing with people two and three times my age. In '77, I was 18. At 19, I won the ASA National Championship--I was the youngest national champion in stock car racing. In the circles that we traveled, I was the youngest and the most outstanding. When I started getting into the national ranks, it was real, real exciting to be younger than everybody else and to be better than most. There was never anything quite like that. That's all different now.

In 1985, I still wanted to be famous. Then in '95, I would have given anything not to be famous. You change. I think nine out of ten people if they had the preference, would do without the fame after they found out what it was. There are a lot of benefits to being famous, but there are also a lot of cons to it. It comes with a lot of debt and responsibility. If I could do what I do and live the life I live and no one knew, I would do it. There was an actor who played with a mask on, so no one knew who he was when he walked down the street; that was a good deal. He did his thing, made his money. All I want in my life now is a little normalcy.

It gets lonesome in this business. You don't get to spend as much time with your family as you might if you came home from work every evening. Working a nine-to-five job isn't glamorous, but it makes for a pretty good family life. Friendship requires a certain amount of maintenance, but in this business, you can't afford a very high maintenance friend. Any high maintenance relationship tends to dissolve. I never had just one specific friend through my years of growing up because I was always on the move and changing directions. I'd have one for a while, then another one for a while, then another one. My friends now are Ernie Irvan, my crew chief, Jimmy Fennig, and the guys who work on my car. That's what it's been for 25 years.

When I retire, I want to have a friend I can spend some quality time with, share camaraderie and the same interests. But if I got a friend now, and he needed me, well, that's tough luck. If someone in my family dies--tough luck. If we have a tragedy in the family, I'm excused because of my job. That was fun for a while, but I look forward to not needing to be excused from all those kinds of things. The grief and tragedy of my dad's accident and my nephew's accident really changed my outlook on things. I don't want my job to stand between me and my personal life.

Right now, my schedule drives me; when I retire, it's going to reverse. I'm going to drive my schedule. I'm still going to go like crazy, but I'm going to be boss of my schedule; I'm a slave to my schedule now. I want to be able to pick and choose, only do what I want to do when I want to do it, and how I want to do it. When you give 30 years to something and you give it your all--every ounce you have had--you've earned the right to do that. When I retire, I don't want to sit on the couch with nowhere to go, nothing to do.

I have dreams. Ten years ago, I had dreams of becoming the Winston Cup Champion. Today, I have dreams beyond that, dreams that are to me more meaningful than even that.

Mark Martin, Max Helton and Ron Camacho

The Seasons in His Life

Autumn 2000 arrived gently in Indiana, and the small tree outside the Indianapolis race shop of Kenny Irwin, Sr. is slowly releasing its grip on the few leaves that remain on its branches. Inside the shop, he sits quietly in his office surrounded by pictures and trophies, each a reminder of the steps his son, Kenny Irwin, Jr., took to reach the top of his sport. The pain, the ever-present pain, still shows in his father's eyes. His voice still breaks between laughter and tears, just as it has since that Friday in July when he heard the news that his son was gone. The racing world was still mourning the death, two months earlier, of Adam Petty. Surely this could not happen again! But it did! In the same turn, on the same track, Kenny Irwin Jr. lost his life on July 7, 2000. His father not only lost his son, he lost his best friend.

Kenny Irwin, Sr. is a man with calloused hands, but not a calloused heart. His eyes, his smile, and his mannerisms show a remarkable resemblance between father and son. He had been a racer, but gave it up to support his family. He learned business the hard way, but chose the road of integrity. His honesty and humility are refreshing and rare in this day and age, and his character is built on hard work, discipline, honesty, and devotion to family. He is a man after God's heart.

Because of his recent loss, he is guarded. Still, there is a transparency and honesty that opens the heart as he speaks, "When Kenny was born in 1969, I had about given up on having a son. My dad had three boys, and I expected boys. Our first child was going to be called Scott. But the first child came along and, since we had a girl, Scott was not a good name. By the time Reva had given birth to two girls I came to expect another girl. I was actually shocked when Reva gave birth to a boy.

"I decided on the day that Kenny was born that if he wanted to race, he was going to. I raced through Kenny," remembers Kenny Sr., as tears start to fill his eyes. "The day before his fourth birthday, Kenny learned to ride a bike and on his birthday, I gave him a 'two-wheeler' mini bike that I had built and cut down. From that moment on he had something motorized to drive.

"When he was five we moved up to quarter midgets and we eventually drove go-carts and road-racecars. I remember when he was 16 he came to me and said 'Dad, I want to make racing my profession,' I will never forget that day. From that moment on I knew that he would give the professional effort that it took to become a successful driver. I just always had a sense that Kenny had what it took. In 1990, we were watching television one night and saw Jeff Gordon racing midget cars at a nearby Raceway Park. I looked over at Kenny and asked, 'Would you like to try that? Do you think you could do that?'

"The next morning I went out and bought our #7 midget car. Jeff Gordon's stepfather, John Bickford, would become my friend and mentor and, if Kenny were here today, he would tell you that Jeff and John played a big part in his success.

"After Kenny won the USAC National Midget Series Championship in 1996, opportunities began to open up. But opportunities are only good if you prove yourself. You not only have to prove you have the ability as a driver, you have to show that you have a personality that is attractive to sponsors and Kenny had a personality that sponsors loved. Kenny received that personality from his mom. You would have to meet Reva and spend a little time with her to see what a remarkable woman she is. She laid the foundation for our home that allowed Kenny to reach the top.

"In 1969 we started going to church," Kenny Sr. states fondly. "We were struggling financially and lived in a small house. Reva always loved church. She grew up in a family that never went to church, but she had a heart for the Lord. She would get up on Sunday morning and get Kim and Kelly ready for church. Pregnant with Kenny, she would have to crawl over me as I slept in on Sundays. I started feeling guilty. Finally, watching Reva's faithfulness, I started going to church with her. When I think about Kenny and where he is, I have a very good feeling. It was because of his mother and her consistent steadiness toward the Lord that Kenny came to know Him. Reva has a long list of people she has touched. Even Jill, Kenny's girlfriend, who never went to church in her life, was saved in our church. Kenny got both good and bad habits through me. Reva had the heart that our children followed." This time the tears are tears of thanks.

"Family is very important to us." A smile comes on Kenny's face as he recalls the family times together. "Holidays are very big in our family. Christmas, birthdays, Thanksgiving, and Easter are celebrated in a special way. To show you how crazy it gets, our son was 30 years old this past Easter and Reva still had Easter egg hunts with Kenny, Kim, Kelly and Korrie and their extended families. She will hide a hundred-dollar bill in one egg and it is a rivalry every year as to who will win the hundred-dollar bill. Can you imagine my over thirty-something children banging heads in an Easter Egg hunt? It was sort of embarrassing to me in a way, but it brought great joy to our family.

"By 1996, Kenny was ready to take the next step in racing when it was offered. He raced the Craftsman Truck Series and did well there with two wins and the Rookie of the Year title. We started hearing that there might be a chance that he could move up to Winston Cup. I remember the phone call I received from Reva, she said, 'Kenny signed with a team. Who do you think it was?'

'Well, I know who I want it to be. I would want it to be the #28 team.'

'Well,' she said, 'That's who he signed with.'

"I was overjoyed. My favorite picture of Kenny is the one of him putting on the Yates team jacket at 'The Brickyard.' I was there with him and that was the proudest day of my life. I wish he could have stayed with the 28 team until he retired, but he had great hopes for the 42 team.

"In the last couple of years Kenny had become a good business manager. He saved almost all that he earned and we inherited his estate. He has put us in a financial position that we have never been in before and it wasn't in our plans. I know that no parent would trade places with us. No parent expects a child to die before they do. It is almost unnatural, but it happens. I look back now and realize that even as Reva was crawling over me to get out of bed for church, God had a plan for Kenny's life. I don't blame myself for Kenny's death or for his choice to become a racecar driver. It was God's timing for Kenny to leave this earth.

I realize with Kenny's passing how much time I spent with Kenny growing up and how little time I spent with the girls. It is a shame to be 55 and have to learn things that should have come naturally. I have not really shown them how much I love them. I cannot fill in the gap of 30 years, but it is important for them to see that they have a dad who loves them. I find myself wanting to do more for my grandchildren. I feel that I now have the opportunity to heal some of the things that I did not do with the girls.

"Kenny's heart touched many, especially children. He loved children. He may have been a man on the outside, but he was a kid on the inside. That is why we established the Kenny Irwin Memorial Foundation. This fund will help children with special needs. We pray that it will be around long after we are gone.

"I still find myself seeking Kenny's approval. I feel like his spirit is watching over me. There was a mutual admiration between us, as well as an accountability for what was right.

"When John Nemechek was killed in the truck accident at Homestead in 1997, I only thought of one thing…that Kenny had won the race. I did not think of what the Nemechek family was going through like I should have. I walked in the house the other day and Reva was talking to John's mother on the phone. Now I can relate and I need to reach out more. I should've done it before. Kyle and Patti Petty have reached out to us through their tragedy. I want to be there for others. When I meet people who are not saved, I stop and I say a prayer for them.

"I had never taken a sleeping pill before the night of Kenny's accident. That was the worst day of my life. It could not get any worse. I felt that if I could go to sleep, I could wake up in the morning and all of this would have been a bad dream. I thought, 'Kenny can't really be gone.' Then I felt the satisfaction of knowing that Kenny was a Christian and that his soul is in heaven. We have to realize that this is just a trial we go through. You have to ask God's forgiveness and ask Him to come into your heart, and then you will be saved. Someday we will wake up in eternity. Compared to eternity, this life is just a vapor."

Kenny Irwin, Sr., Brad Winters and Ron Camacho

Any donations to the Kenny Irwin Memorial Foundation can be sent directly to 5338 Victory Drive, Indianapolis, IN 46203.

Lost Your Job? Humpy's Phone Calls

His phone call to the recently fired or laid off always begins this way: "It's Humpy Wheeler. I heard you lost your job. What can I do to help?" He listens with his heart first, in a way that only someone who has been there can. "I'll tell you what someone told me many years ago," he begins. "When trouble comes, make a plan to move ahead and never, ever look back." And that, is when he tells this story:

"I've had to restart my life in a major way three times. The first was the University of South Carolina and I was playing football down there and I broke my back. I couldn't play anymore and so I had to shift from a physical to a mental focus at that point.

"The second time, was at Charlotte Motor Speedway, which is now Lowe's Motor Speedway, in 1960. Bruton Smith, who is now chairman of the board, got fired himself in 1960 by the trustees because the track went into bankruptcy. There just wasn't enough money up front. I got fired from what is now Lowe's Motor Speedway in 1963. I never did figure out why. But I was only about 24 years old and it was devastating.

"Then, I was with Firestone for seven years but they got out of the racing business and so I lost that position and I had to start all over again. So, I have a lot of empathy for people when they hit an oak tree.

"When I got fired, I leased the Concord Speedway and started running the dirt track races again, which is what I started off doing. Sometimes you have to go backwards to make forward progress. I had a family and I lost all the money I had. I had to move out of

Charlotte and move to Ohio and work up there, but I gained a lot in the process. I promise that in every setback, you can make forward progress.

"The early years of my life I was around Belmont Abbey a lot--the monastery part of it. I have a great deal of thankfulness and admiration for the Benedictine monks because they believe very strongly In the vow of humility. I think you have to remain humble and, just because you've gotten somewhere in life, you are no more important than anyone else. When I wake up in the morning I try to never think of myself as an important person. If I ever do start thinking that way, I remind myself of all the mistakes I STILL make.

"I just have great empathy for particularly talented people when they lose their job. It's probably the lowest ebb that any one can get to--outside of divorce or death in the family. It's just a time when people really need to get picked up. I know this from experience, so I just call people when I know they're going through it.

"My advice is don't get mad and don't beat yourself up. Take every bit of that energy that you would spend on those negative thoughts and put it all into positive action so that you can get another job or find another career. The key is keeping a forward outlook, and that's very hard to do. Don't look back. If you've made a mistake that has cost you your job, then you can learn something from it--that is if you'll admit the mistake to yourself.

"I find that most people lose their jobs because they are at the wrong place at the wrong time. It's personally devastating, even then. A lot of people don't realize that. They start thinking, 'If I had been a better 'this' or a better 'that' I would still have my job.' I've seen talented people lose their job while incompetent people stay, simply for the fact that we have a lot of incompetent top management. That's something people don't talk much about. So, you can get your head messed up in that and you just cannot allow that to happen. I know. I've been there, and maybe that's why I try to make those phone calls."

Claire B. Lang

H. A. "Humpy" Wheeler is now the president of Lowe's Motor Speedway, the very speedway he was fired from thirty years ago.

Green 18

Kimberly Schneider was two years old when her chubby knees turned bright red. "She wasn't falling down all the time as the doctors first thought," her mother, racing journalist Jane Smith recalls, "But her knees were just the brightest red you have ever seen." It took a succession of specialists and six years of medial tests before doctors were finally able to diagnose the problem. Kimberly, they said, had not one, but two chronic diseases: scleroderma, a form of arthritis, and dermatomyositis, better know as muscular dystrophy.

"She was in for a long, hard road," Smith sighs. "We all were." While some families pull together in times of crisis, others are strained to the breaking point. Kimberly's fell into the latter category. Unable to handle the daily struggle, her father deserted his family. At that point, Smith packed up and moved her children to Merritt Island, Florida.

"Kimberly spent the first part of her elementary school years in a wheelchair, never being involved in P. E. or any outside activities," Smith remembers. "But little by little, her doctors at Shands Hospital in Gainesville found medicine that strengthened her muscles and kept her diseases in check. By the time she was ten, she no longer needed the wheelchair."

During this time, Smith--a huge racing fan-- introduced her children to the sport. "First we started out at the local drag strip," she recalls. "But then one weekend, we checked out Orlando Speedworld, a circle track close to the drag strip. That was it! We were hopelessly hooked on round track racing. And

THEN we discovered NASCAR racing on TV.

"From that very first race, Kimberly picked out one young driver that somehow impressed her more than the others--Bobby LaBonte," Smith continues. "Whatever Booby had, she loved. She wanted to race like him. Why? To prove she could do it because she was told she couldn't.

"And guess what--she did it! This young woman who had spent her early childhood in a wheelchair got out there and raced with the guys and held her own simply because Bobby LaBonte, the man in Green 18, led the way for her.

"Every time Kimberly got into her 1971 Buick Regal Runabout to race, she put on the dashboard a small model of LaBonte's number 18 car," Smith says. "That model car traveled many racing circuits with her--giving her the strength to prove to herself and the world that anything in this life is achievable if you want it bad enough.

"Sometimes the heroes in our lives never know they are heroes. LaBonte may not know it, but he gave my daughter the confidence to spread her wings and fly."

Jane Smith

Toothpick Philosophy

When I came to this country from my homeland of Cuba in the early '60's, I didn't speak any English. I had only $25.00 and two boxes of cigars to my name. I sold the cigars at the airport in Miami to help raise some money for my new adventure here. I didn't come from an impoverished family, but I came here to make my own way. I was determined to make a success of myself. I held various odd jobs, from washing cars to working in a furniture factory. I lived in a lot of different fleabag hotels and in boarding rooms. In Lexington, North Carolina I once lived in an abandoned funeral home that the Catholic Church helped me convert into a home for my mother, my brother, and my sister when they came here from Cuba.

After I married my wife, Carolyn, she convinced me that I would be a good salesman and I answered a blind ad in the paper. The ad turned out to be a car sales position with a Chrysler dealership. That was in 1963 and, within one year, I was their number one salesman. Some time later I got a job working for a man who had known my father in Cuba. I had sold him a couple of cars and he hired me to come to work for his company. Within three years, I bought the company from him. From there I got involved with the World of Wonders Toy Company, the Atari Company, and various other enterprises. My company was the first company to get involved with taking Compaq computers into the retail market. My company also got involved with Rick Hendrick in the founding of a new basketball team, the Charlotte Hornets.

Rick Hendrick helped me to get involved in actually buying into a racing team. My wife is from North

Carolina and has always loved NASCAR racing. We had attended many races with her family and I loved the sport. When they start up the engines and drop the green flag, it gives you a rush that is hard to describe. Being around the garage area and working with the teams is one of the things I love the most about it. You get so close to the people there. One of the hardest things about that is when you lose people like Adam Petty. His dad, Kyle, had driven for me for years and I had watched Adam grow up. Adam had driven one of our Legend cars. Another sad loss was when Alan Kulwicki died. My whole family was really close to Alan and we still miss him. Then we lost Kenny Irwin. I didn't know him as well, but these losses really changed the direction I took with my team.

I have always tried to surround myself with successful people. These associations have helped me to become the success that I am today. They have helped me to have the opportunity to share in a sport that I love with people of great courage and fortitude. I will always remember what my grandfather told me when I was leaving Cuba. He told me that Americans don't like to associate with people who are unsuccessful. He said, "If you are hungry, put a toothpick in your mouth so that people will think that you have just finished a huge steak. Never let them know you are hungry." I never give up on anything. I do whatever I have to do to be a winner and whatever combination I have to make to do that, I'm going to do it.

Felix Sabates and Ron Camacho

"I Gave It All I Had"

The old sedan careened at breakneck speed down the winding, hilly back roads of Arkansas. Steep corners and lanky pine trees appeared out of nowhere. Five-year-old Mark Martin desperately steered around them, trying to rein in the thunderous, eight-cylindered machine. Drenched in sweat and terrified, he set his jaw and with blazing intensity, focused on his steering and the narrow, battered road ahead. His sheer will held the car to the course.

Abruptly, the sedan lost power. Julian Martin, with Mark still standing between his legs, took his foot off the accelerator and let the footloose auto slow to a crawl. He grinned at his young son, pulled him onto his lap and rumpled his hair. He was proud of Mark and knew he'd taught him a valuable lesson: how to succeed against all odds. Second-best didn't count. Either you gave it all you had or you failed.

His father's frequent, often brutal, tests of courage bred in Mark Martin an intense, determined streak that has never left him. Despite all the bad decisions Julian made in his life--the drinking, the divorces, and the wild and nearly suicidal lifestyle--Mark still unflaggingly idolized his father. To this day, he attributes his whole success as one of NASCAR's premiere marquee drivers to the devotion and discipline imparted upon him by Julian Martin.

On August 16, 1998, the NASCAR Winston Cup Series was in Michigan to run the Pepsi 400. Mark was there, too, but his spirit was in anguish. The previous week, Julian Martin had taken his wife, Shelley, and his daughter, Sarah, for a ride in his private plane. Somewhere short of their destination, the plane plummeted to the ground, killing all three instantly.

It was a crushing blow for Mark. And yet, the drive to persevere--the intensity that Julian had hammered into his psyche over the years--demanded that he put his feelings aside and do his duty for his race team. Julian was dead, Mark's world was in chaos, and yet he still had a race to win.

Mark was overwhelmed by reporters trying to get the scoop on how he felt, wondering if his father's death might motivate him to succeed. He managed to muster up a few smiles, offered a few standard replies to their callous questions, but refused to give any of them the outward emotion they expected. He simply delivered what he always did--Mark Martin, quiet and noncommittal. That is, until the final moment before the window net went up in his #6 Valvoline Ford.

"There is no one more motivated to win than I am," he succinctly told the press. The flinty hardness in his eyes, the rock-hard set to his jaw, and his deadly intensity betrayed the agonizing forces at work within him that weekend. No one doubted that he meant every word. And no one could argue with his actions on the track.

From the word go, the #6 Valvoline Ford was on a tear. Instead of his usual pattern of hanging around the top five and saving the car until the last half of the race, Mark seemed to be channeling the hell-for-leather spirit of his father as he battled pole-sitter Ernie Irvan for the lead. Sometimes going three or four wide in lapped traffic, letting his car zoom toward the wall like he was intent on taking it down, using teammate Kevin Lepage as a pick to pass Irvan for the lead--Mark's determination and competitive fire was almost frightening to watch. It was almost as if he were back on Julian's lap in that old pickup truck, desperately determined to please his father by besting those unforgiving, twisting Arkansas roads.

With twenty laps to go, Mark held the lead. But at lap 185, a scant 30 miles from the checkered flag, a caution bunched up on the field. The Roush Racing pit crew got Mark out ahead of everyone else just as they had been doing most of the day, but lurking in third was Mark's points-race nemesis, Jeff Gordon.

Gordon and the #24 team had been uncharacteristically out of contention all day. In fact, few expected Gordon, who would go on to win the 1998 championship, to be a serious contender in the Pepsi 400. But thanks to fast pit work, Gordon and the DuPont car were within reach of Mark and second-place Dale Jarrett during the final caution. When the green fell, Jeff Gordon blew around both Jarrett and Mark like they were tied to tree stumps. Gordon led his first (and last) nine laps of the event, simply driving away from everyone. He cruised to an easy victory, utterly destroying what had been turning into the Cinderella story of the day.

Mark was devastated by the loss. He'd poured his whole heart and soul into this race, at times driving like a man possessed. To be so close to a victory--a triumphant victory for his father--only to have it snatched away by Gordon's team, was a crushing defeat.

Though Jeff Gordon was taking his bows as the race winner, most eyes were on Mark Martin's red, white, and blue Ford as it slowly moved to pit road. Mark stopped briefly to congratulate Gordon's crew chief, Ray Evernham, then wheeled the #6 straight back to the garage area. Not surprisingly, the media was there to greet him.

Fresh from his defeat, with the weight of the week bearing down on him, Mark could no longer contain his emotions. As he stepped from the car, his usual reserve and aloof demeanor were simply overwhelmed by his sense that he had failed the man he so loved. In the face of a forest of microphones and a glaring blaze of camera flashes, staring down at the asphalt as if to borrow strength from its solidity, Martin gave voice to his anguish.

"Well, we didn't win it," he said, voice trembling. "I gave it my best. I'd like to dedicate that losing performance to my dad, to Shelley, and to Sarah..." Then he raised his head, his eyes cast towards the sky, almost in supplication to the father who had been taken from him. "I gave it all I had."

Tony Johns

Deciding Factor

We built jalopies in our backyard when I was growing up in Lakeland, Florida--a very humble beginning you might say. We built stuff in our backyards and did some good, old-fashioned, down-home renovation with some junkyard parts, and then we got in there and raced all the dirt and asphalt tracks.

I actually started out racing motorcycles, but I figured I'd quit that while I still had all my arms and legs. We put together a motley crew of family and friends to run the family stock for the first few years starting in 1984. My uncles, Jack and Robert, were just in it for fun. They'd sit in the back of their pickup trucks, drink Old Milwaukee and have a good time while I raced their cars.

The most fun I ever had was back in the early years on the dirt tracks when the cars were cheap and came from the junkyard. It wasn't scripted and it wasn't like walking through a minefield. You didn't have to watch what you said or how you looked because you weren't representing big corporate people. It was just "race like blazes and may the best man win!" It's different now because the farther you move up in the business, the more it becomes "business." There are so many more elements now--marketing, politics, and big money.

At the end of last year, I signed a contract with Kool Seal, Inc. This whole ordeal with the ARA (American Racing Association) has been kind of a rush with signing the contract, figuring out our market and coming up with our plan. The ARA is sort of a spin-off of the NASCAR late model stock cars. John Huffman has the Hickory Motor Speedway, Tri-County Motor Speedway, Lonesome Pine, Florida Speed Park and Peach State Speedway, and Montgomery Motor Speedway. We visit three times during a 16-race deal with national points titles.

I've seen a lot of very trying times and hard challenges. I had to be apart from my wife for two of the first four years we were married. I slept on a shop floor and literally bummed meals from friends so that I could fulfill commitments to car owners. I've had some hard knocks, had plenty of doors slammed in my face and rugs snatched out from under me. I've been promised the world and followed a trail that led to nowhere except disappointment.

One of the most painful experiences of my life was being a thousand miles away from my wife, Cindy Kay, when my son, Chase, was born. We were living in Atlanta and really didn't know where my career was headed at that point. We sacrificed everything to pursue our dream, but it wasn't enough. In 1993, Cindy left to live with her mother in Michigan and to birth our son, Chase. It was the toughest thing we ever did. Looking back, I wonder how in the world we did it, but we got through it. My whole family pushed me and they gave me the belief and support I needed at that time, but Cindy was the backbone of that support system.

We met in 1985 during Spring Break at Daytona Beach. We were just kids back then and I had just started racing. She went back to her home in Michigan and we maintained a long-distance relationship. We saw each other a few more times and she wrote to me a lot. I admit I wasn't very good at that, but we stayed in touch over the next few years. We saw each other in Atlanta in 1991 and I decided she was pretty special. I talked to my mom about it and, soon after, Cindy moved to Atlanta and we got married. Now here we are, working on eight years of marriage. I think it's pretty wild!

Chase is our son, and I've got two other children. I guess you could say I was kind of a wild guy and pretty popular back in Florida. My oldest son, Kyle, lives with us, and my daughter, Hope, lives in Florida with her mom. Cindy is so awesome. She raised Kyle, coached him in T-ball and the whole she-bang. She's incredible. I couldn't have dreamed up a better person to share my life. Sometimes I wonder what I did so special that God smiled on me and gave me Cindy.

In 1996, I was driving for Ray Everett in Wilson, North Carolina and was sponsored by Wendy's. We won a lot of races and I still hold the track speed record from Southern National Speedway in 1996, but we lost everything. I lost my house, my business and, for the second time in our marriage, Cindy had to move back to Michigan--this time with both of the two younger children. I slept on the couch in my shop with my dog. When school let out, my son, Kyle, joined me for the rest of the year. We went to our friend's house, raided their cabinets and ate cereal so that I could fulfill my commitment to my sponsor and car owner. That's when Barry Graham, with the Richard Petty Driving Experience, called and wanted me to come to Charlotte and be a driving instructor. I was holding back when Cindy called from Michigan and said she had a dream about me living in Charlotte among the other professional racers and being very successful. She said I belonged there. Apparently it was a pretty powerful dream. She felt so strongly about it that she refused to come back to North Carolina unless I packed my bags and met her in Charlotte. She told me, "You belong in Charlotte, and I'm not coming back unless you go there." Well, that tipped the scale of my decision making process! The Richard Petty Driving Experience didn't seem like a big deal to me, but I knew it would look good on my resume and after Cindy's call, I moved to Charlotte. All I had was my truck and my tools.

In the fall of 1996, Cindy's mom had helped us buy a little mobile home, but it wouldn't be ready until the summer of 1997. I found us a place to rent in the meantime, and Cindy and the boys finally came back in January 1997. For a long time I wondered, "Why am I here?"

When we got the mobile home set-up, Cindy and her mom went out to get some Kool Seal to coat the metal roof on it. I got to looking at the addresses on the bottom of the can. I called information and got the phone number for Kool Seal, Inc. out of Twinsburg, Ohio. Next thing you know I had Steve Hudak, the president of the company, on the phone! We corresponded for almost two years.

About a year ago, I was pretty comfortable with the idea of just being a husband and a dad. I've got two sons who race carts. My nine-year old is really awesome! I've been racing for 16 years and, to tell the truth, I've taken a beating. I was just so tired and worn out, I really contemplated letting it all go. Then, the deal with Kool Seal came through, and I knew I was in the right place at the right time.

I've always had a strong faith. My mom and dad instilled that inner force. That force stays with me, telling me to keep going and pushing me forward. There were times when I felt like I was at a dead end, but for some reason, I just had to keep going. I'd be bleeding, sweating and crying, but that force in me told me to hang on and keep trying to reach that next open door. I think that everybody's got a special gift to contribute. Sometimes, when I see a bum, I think, "Why can't that guy see what his gift is?" Is it that only a selected minority have that something special to offer? There were times when I would look in the mirror and think, "What a shame. There's something more that I'm supposed to be." But because of the faith, I struggled to make it happen; I never quit pushing, and that's what brought me here today.

I don't know where all this is going to take me, but I know this: My goal is to be more, to be a better person tomorrow than I am today, to go as far as I can, to do as much as I can, and be as much I can be when it's all said and done. Every day for me is a learning thing--a growth thing. Life doesn't owe me anything, and believing that makes everything easier to handle. Sometimes the elements in life don't seem fair, but if I was naked in the desert tomorrow, I know I'd make it.

It is my belief that winning is a matter of choice because, even in failure, you can still win. It's all about how you handle it, how you overcome it. Even failure can be the best opportunity for growth because the door is wide open for you then. How you go through that door is the deciding factor of whether you win or lose.

Greg Davis

The Long Road

Matching Scars

Growing up in Midland, Texas, I was very active and involved in lots of fun stuff, which sometimes got me in trouble. I have several scars to prove it! I almost died of typhoid fever when I was five years old. I was in the hospital for three weeks, but they didn't know what was wrong with me. (Typhoid fever was an unheard of disease in the United States.) Finally, the lady who had been babysitting me told them she was a carrier of typhoid fever. Once they knew what it was, they treated it. But it was a pretty touchy situation for a while.

When I was eight, I was run over by a station wagon. The front and back tires ran over me and took my ear half off. It also took a little chunk out of the left side of my leg. They had to do surgery on my stomach to check out everything on the inside. I've got some major scars from that. It was a pure miracle that I lived.

Then, when I was ten years old, I began having pain in my leg at night. I couldn't sleep well because it got so severe. I'd go back to my mom and dad, who would rub my leg. I would finally get to sleep, only to wake up after a few minutes. I was only getting two to three hours of sleep at night because it was hurting so badly. I got it x-rayed, but they couldn't find anything wrong with it until I went back to the doctor a year later. Sure enough, this time he discovered that I had a tumor in the bone. He immediately scheduled surgery.

In order to reach the tumor, the surgeon had to strip away the calf muscle, saw the leg in half in two different places, then let it grow back together again. After cutting through the muscle to the bone, the doctor couldn't find anything wrong with the leg. He looked up at the chart and realized he'd made a terrible mistake--HE HAD CUT THE WRONG LEG! He had to sew it back up and start over on the other one. Fortunately, he was luckier on his second try: he found the tumor and got all of it. When I woke up, I had a big cast on one leg and a bandage on the other leg. The bones eventually healed, but I now have two scars--one going down each leg. As an eleven-year-old kid, I thought it was pretty cool because my legs matched. It healed pretty quickly because I was young.

Beneath the scars, I mended both physically and emotionally, nurtured by a very supportive father. My dad and I were, and still are, very close. He instilled a tough, West Texas mindset in me that helped me endure the pain of my early mishaps. Even though my folks never took me to church, they would tell me, "God must have something special in store for you after all you've survived." They were right. In the midst of enduring, sometimes unbearable pain, I learned the healing power of forgiveness.

When I was 21, I joined a Christian organization called "Young Life." I knew God wanted me to live for Him. I learned a lot about Him through this organization and knew that I needed Him in my life, but I didn't accept Him until later. I met Lake Speed and his wife when I started racing. They would have me over to their place for dinner and we would read the Bible together. It was through my relationship with them that I finally surrendered my life to Christ. It's difficult living a Christian life, but the reward--the peace that He gives to those who truly make Him Lord of their lives--is well worth it. A lot of people have misconceptions, thinking it's easy. It's a responsibility. He sets a standard that we try to live and operate by. It's not easy. When I first started racing, I wanted to be the meanest, toughest, "baddest" driver out there. God changed all of that. He had a different plan for me. When I realized that and got right with God, it was literally a new life.

Lake Speed, Daryl Waltrip, their wives, my wife, Kim, and I began a ministry at the races for other drivers, but it was hit and miss. When I heard that Max Helton was going to leave for Tampa, Florida to live, I told him that a couple of us were going to start a ministry in Charlotte. Max wasn't pastoring a church and was pretty much on his own, so he started coming out and doing Bible studies with us. He had the vision for this ministry, so he laid it out for us and it just grew into what the Motor Racing Outreach (MRO) is today. Max is now chaplain of the MRO.

How you sail through the storms in life is what counts. I'm going through a storm right now. We are selling our race team. I don't have a job for next year, but I've been in this position before and God has always provided. He has a plan for me; it's just a matter of exercising my faith, which stands as an example to other people. It's when we go through tough times that keeping the faith gets challenging. For example, I have a young friend here. We prayed together and he received Christ. He was terribly frustrated one day and finally blurted out, "You'd think if God wanted to use you He would have you winning a bunch of races so you could tell people about Him." I said, "Yeah, but if I won a bunch of races, people would think that's the only reason I praise Christ. When I can praise Him in tough times, then people know it's real."

Bobby Hillin, Jr.

CHAPTER SIX
The Fans

"...As you get older, it is harder to have heroes, but it is sort of necessary."
Ernest Hemingway

"I want to do it my way. I don't mind the hard work and I enjoy the challenge. If I succeed, I've done it myself. If I fail, well, I can say I tried." Alan Kulwicki

He Did It His Way

My first experience with NASCAR was when I was dating my husband. We lived in Arizona and the only contact with "race cars" was with local drag racing back in my hometown of Indiana. I thought NASCAR would be boring just watching the cars go around and around. That misconception was quickly pushed aside when I found myself cheering on a guy I didn't know anything about.

The only reason I started cheering him was because of the number on his car, and his last name. I'm of Polish decent, and to find a racecar driver of the same decent made it seem fated to root for him. The number of his car was also my "lucky" number since I was born on the 7th day of the 7th month. Thus, my connection with Alan Kulwicki was born. My enthusiasm for the sport and for watching a phenomenal driver only increased with each race.

My husband, Art, was thrilled that I was interested in a sport that he had enjoyed for years. When I saw Alan win and do a "Polish Victory" lap, I was all choked up. I saw him as someone who embraced his heritage and wasn't afraid to make light of it with a gesture that really was a better way of showing the fans his appreciation by getting closer to them. To this day, I get tears in my eyes when other drivers do the Polish Victory lap. They are showing tribute to a man who wasn't afraid to be a trailblazer.

Throughout the years, I was in awe of how Alan accomplished so much in such a short time. Not only was he an owner/driver, he took care of the business primarily by himself. He was probably a "control freak" to his colleagues, but to us, he showed a determination and drive to succeed that is hard to find in people these days. His work ethic, alone, made him an excellent role model for anyone. His engineering degree brought new technology to the sport and showed others that you didn't have to have a father in the business to succeed. His Polish heritage and being a Yankee made him an underdog in this primarily Southern sport. His little mascot, "Mighty Mouse," seemed to explain everything about Alan Kulwicki. He was a minority in a "Good-ole-boys" game, but he was definitely a force to be reckoned with.

In 1992, when he won the Winston Cup Championship, it seemed like the basic rules we are taught as children really were true...Good does prevail and working hard does lead to success. When they played, "I Did it My Way" while the film of that year rolled on the screen during the awards, I felt great pride and joy for a man that I was honored to meet, but never was fortunate enough to know. It was as though a member of my family was up there accepting an award. My husband and I were able to see the last race he was in at Darlington. He didn't have a very successful race, but we enjoyed the excitement of being there anyway.

When we got back home to Oklahoma, we were devastated when we heard the news of the plane crash and of his death. It was like a member of the family had died. We were getting calls from friends and family from all over the country to ask us if we heard the tragic news and to see how we were taking it.

All the time we are told about famous people dying, but never has it made such an impact on my life as when Alan Kulwicki died. It was hard to watch a race and not cry. When the winners would say, "This one's for Alan," it would bring up the sadness and tears all over again. It took the whole of the 1993 season to get over. Over the years, we still don't have a "favorite" driver that we follow with the same enthusiasm.

We still watch and enjoy the sport, but it just isn't the same. Perhaps it's because we haven't seen the same conviction or will to succeed, despite the odds, from the other drivers. Maybe it's just because there will never be another Alan Kulwicki that was strong-willed enough to drive his car "backwards" around the track when he won, and because no matter what, HE DID IT HIS WAY.

Karen Fenrich

The Finish Line Decides

If you had asked me three years ago to tell you what the "Winston Cup" was I might have guessed hockey or horse racing. I had never seen or heard of the term before January 4, 1997. On that fateful day, all aspects of my life changed forever. On that day, I received an e-mail from my father, who I had never met in my 27 years of life.

After the initial shock and tears, we spoke on the phone about our favorite pastimes and he said the magic words, "You ever watch car racing?" I, an anti-sports fanatic, was skeptical. However, looking for some common ground with this unfamiliar man, I agreed to watch the Daytona 500 from green flag to checkers. I was surprisingly impressed.

At my father's prompting, I chose a "favorite" driver (completely at random) to add to the excitement. Now, he's an Earnhardt man, so I wasn't allowed to choose him, although I liked Dale's style. So, I chose the other Dale, whom I read "showed promise." Thus began the Sunday Saga that has brought my father and I together as nothing ever could--friendly competition! Each week, my father in Florida and I in California, watch the race. We know that the weekly telephone call will conclude our bet. No matter who wins, if Dale Earnhardt finished ahead of Dale Jarrett, it's my dime, and if the 88 beats the 3, I await the happiest sounds of all--the jingle of the telephone and the sound of my father's voice on the other end.

Kira Bloomingdale

NASCAR Sure Beats Vacuum Cleaners

For those of us rabid NASCAR fans who are old enough to remember Richard Petty racing, but don't remember Lee, we're likely to be dealing with the teenage-years of our children; and trying to do it with all the wisdom, patience, and diplomacy we can muster (especially when our kids ask if we ever got really drunk and stupid). I was a little older than some when I had Josh--I was twenty-eight, and God in His infinite wisdom knew I needed a little more time to let life trample over me and toughen me up. He knew He was giving me quite a 'special' little boy, and I was going to need all the life's experience I could stuff in my head and my heart.

Joshua was a wild one before he was born, constantly pushing his foot against my ribs in an effort that was, I swear, an attempt to break out of his warm and wet little jail. He sent me into premature labor five or six times before the doctor finally broke away the dam and let him loose, two weeks early. He hasn't stopped since. We've picked up some medical diagnoses along the way: some they call "learning disabilities"—also known as "a-lazy-parent's-excuse-to-drug-a-kid-into-submission:" but you get the idea. I know you've heard of ADHD. He's got that one, as well as ODD, PDD, OCD, and Asperger's Syndrome. It's unlikely you've heard of most of these. Be glad, and thank your God in heaven. To make the mix as volatile as possible, throw in a neurological disorder known as "Tourette Syndrome." I'll bet you think this is "The Swearing Disorder." You're misinformed, but I don't have time to teach you about it here.

Joshua thinks about things a lot differently than most and, as long as he stays proud of it, this will take him far in the world. I know that whatever he does, he'll do it a thousand times better, and with a million times more creativity than a lot of others. He says he's going to be a NASCAR driver; but if his tics hold him back from that (and they shouldn't; they should wane and leave him when he's ready to jump in the window of that racecar), he's going to be an announcer. Let me tell you, he uses the little racecars we fight other adults for in Wal-Mart and K-Mart, to put on a race. He can use that racing lingo as smoothly and impressively as Benny Parsons. He's getting to know all the stats on all the drivers, too. Besides his boyish voice, you'd think Buddy Baker, or Dr. Jerry Punch was right in your kitchen, down on the floor announcing the most exciting race NASCAR ever had. When Joshua showed an interest in NASCAR, we nourished and nurtured this into the passion that it is today. In the past, he'd rejected more normal boyhood thoughts and developed an obsession with vacuum cleaners. Did we go to the toy department? No, we went to where they line up the vacuum cleaners, and sometimes let you turn them on. It was a special day for my boy when they let him push around the Eurekas. We've even had him to a few races. If I weren't such a fanatical Jeff Burton fan, I'd spend my race time watching Joshua watch the race. You can read on his face if his favorite, Bobby Labonte, is near the front or not. And, if by chance Bobby loses an engine or gets shoved into a wall, Joshua will root for the underdogs. In his races he holds in the kitchen, Stacey, Kenny, Jerry, and others like them all win regularly; it's a joyous time they have in the Winner's

Circle--Joshua sees to it.

Because there are a few people in our community who don't understand my son and his disorders, his friends are few and his social life isn't what it should be. But NASCAR has filled that void, and then some. We've got the flags, hats, T-shirts, bumper stickers, and everything else related. But you should see his face, his shining face, when the green number 18 takes the lead. Oh, how he laughs, and jumps off the couch, and is just so dang HAPPY! You should hear the funny things he mutters when Bobby isn't doing so good. And what it meant to him when he got an autographed picture in the mail from Jerry Nadeau (an event that occurred thanks to Sue, a REAL angel)! "He wrote something personal to ME, Mom! It's to ME! Joshua Walker!" Am I going to be a NASCAR fan forever? Is the mud red around Martinsville?

Cheryl Walker

Camp Good Days

For several years, I have coordinated a visit to Watkins Glen Racetrack for the kids at "Camp Good Days and Special Times." The children who attended this camp were all undergoing treatments for various types of cancer. I would get collectibles from the different teams and other sources for the kids, as well as some other types of activity related to racing at the track.

The last year I was able to coordinate this event for the kids, I had lined up Benny Parsons, road course driver Scott Lagasse, as well as a friend of mine who drove at the local track, Chris Morris. With the line up of celebrities and some great limited edition Mattel Hot Wheels to give away, I knew this was going to be a good event. Chris and Scott had their cars there and we set them up on the playground for the kids to see and get into. We took pictures of the kids sitting in the cars, as well as handing out whatever collectibles the kids wanted. The kids and counselors alike were in awe of the sounds of the cars and we were all having a great time.

Out of all the kids, two in particular stood out that afternoon. One was from Europe and was blind due to a brain tumor. The other had lost his leg due to bone cancer. The child from Europe couldn't get enough of the cars. Even though he couldn't see them, he seemed to be enthralled with the chance to sit behind the wheel and fire up the engine. His doctor told me that the boy had always wanted to drive a car some day, but knew it wasn't going to happen. This was almost as good as fulfilling that dream. He took his Hot

Wheel's collectible and imitated the sound of the engine of a real racecar, driving it all over the camp.

The other boy had been going through treatment for well over a year in hopes of putting the cancer into remission. Over the winter, he lost his leg to the cancer and had been in a depressed state ever since. When he came to the camp that summer, he was withdrawn and unwilling to participate in any event. When he got to the track, he was at first reluctant to approach the cars or take the collectibles we were giving away. When the engines of the cars were started up, he began to warm to our urgings to come look at the cars and try on the helmets. With some coaxing, we finally got him to sit in one of the cars. For the first time in two weeks, he was smiling, laughing and talking with everyone. We captured a picture of the once sullen little boy smiling from ear to ear.

Several weeks after our outing, I spoke with the coordinator of the camp and she informed me that the blind boy had been the center of attention when he had returned home with this great experience to share with everyone. Word from his doctor was that the boy's spirits were higher than he had ever seen. The second boy's experience carried over through the rest of his stay at the camp. His spirits, as well, had remained high. Two young lives were made brighter because of that special encounter with three kind-hearted drivers who turned their sadness into Camp Good Days.

Jim Rosati

The Fans

"I realized I better enjoy and appreciate and contribute as much as I can today because all of this could be gone tomorrow."
Davey Allison

A Hero Forever

Bryan was born on February 18, 1985, after Bill Elliott won the fastest Daytona 500 ever. Perhaps that influenced his choice of NASCAR racing as his favorite sport, not to mention that it is also his parent's passion. Growing up in Alabama, less than two hours from Talladega doesn't hurt either. The local short track was considered "his" racetrack and Talladega was for the grown ups.

Bryan attended his first race at Talladega in 1989 and amazed those around us with the level of knowledge he had for one so young. He knew most of the drivers and their cars, but Davey Allison was his favorite. Davey was young and going full speed ahead. Bryan had already met him, as Davey was an avid hunter and attended the Buckmasters Classic near our home. The Classic was a perfect opportunity for all the kids to meet their favorite heroes, be it from racing, baseball, football, or some other sport. Bryan's favorite was always Davey. Unlike some of the other athletes, Davey would spend time with the kids. Bryan would follow him around like a little puppy. At one Classic, in which Richard Petty was scheduled to attend, Bryan found Davey, put his hands on his hips and asked, "So, Davey, where's Richard?" Davey, with his usual smirk, explained that Linda Petty had gotten sick and Richard wouldn't make it. Bryan's reply: "Okay, then you'll have to do this time." Davey just smiled even more.

Another time, prior to a July race at Talladega, we surprised Bryan by taking him to the FanFest in Anniston. It just so happened that the race fell one week after Davey's horrific crash at Pocono. Unfortunately, he was not able to attend. However, while we were there, it was announced that Davey had been released from the hospital that afternoon. It was not a good FanFest for "Ole D.W.," as everyone was blaming him for the accident. Liz Allison did make the festival on behalf of her husband and spoke to us all. Bryan was lucky enough to win a prize from among all of those gathered there, and it thrilled him beyond belief to be able to climb up on the back of a flatbed trailer and receive his prize from Liz.

Then came that horrible day in June of 1993. Bryan's grandfather had died in May of that year. Although Bryan was upset and cried a lot at the time, we knew he did not completely understand the concept of death. On that day, both he and his parents would learn what it meant to have a child's hero taken from them. We had watched the New Hampshire race and laughed at Davey's comments following the race. His kids had told him that he had better say, "Hi!" Little did any of us know then that we would never hear him talk to us again. I got the news while I was at work, as my boss was as big a NASCAR fan as I was. I picked Bryan up from school, not wanting to tell him about the accident until we got home. I told him that there had been a helicopter accident and that Davey was in the hospital in Birmingham. Bryan asked if he could send a get-well card and I told him of course. He proceeded to get out his crayons and draw the 28 Texaco Ford Havoline car and put get well messages all over it. We made a special trip to the post office that afternoon so that Davey would get it in a hurry. Bryan didn't want to waste time. The next day it was announced that life support was removed and Davey was dead. Bryan was devastated. His only thought was that Davey didn't get his card in time. Whenever the news mentioned Davey's name over the next several days, Bryan could not contain himself. Those lips would pucker and then the tears would flow. He just couldn't look at any pictures or hear his name called on the TV.

We decided that the best way to handle the situation was to let Bryan say good-bye. He dressed in his Sunday best clothes for school on the day of the memorial service. We checked him out of school early and headed for Birmingham. As we got to the church, there were hundreds of people waiting in line. These were people who had grown up with Davey, his neighbors, his church family, and his fans. We saw many drivers there, and I am proud to say that no one bothered them with the trivial things fans normally request. We were all there for a reason and that was to honor Davey and his life. Bryan asked for an orange, gold, and black ribbon and he wrote "28" on construction paper and we pinned it to his shirt. As we got closer to the church entrance, I explained to Bryan that he would not be able to see Davey. He was one of the youngest people there. Upon entering the church, a young man leaned down to Bryan, who by this time was in tears, and asked him if he was a fan of Davey's. Bryan answered yes and said, "He was my friend, too," as if he had known him closely all of his life. The young man smiled and told him Davey would be glad he was there. All the time, I wanted to protect my child, yet as we approached the casket, Bryan patiently waited his turn. He walked by himself up to the beautiful wood structure, with Davey's picture in a frame. This little eight year old put his hands at his side, standing at military attention, and just waited there in quiet meditation for two or three minutes. No one dared to rush him through the line. All by himself, he made his peace and said his goodbyes. I don't know if the Allison's even saw him, as they were not in the public area. But if they did, they had to be proud of this little boy, as I was so proud of him.

As we exited the chapel and got outside, Bryan stopped, looked up at us and said, "Mama, I'm okay now." A little boy had grown up that day. He had the pleasure of meeting his hero in life, which is something not everyone gets a chance to do; he also had the opportunity to let his hero go, to tell him goodbye. Granted, it still hurt for a long time. That first Daytona 500 without Davey was devastating for our family. We cried most of the time, watching that 28 car without Davey driving. However, this past November Bryan was also able to finally close the chapter on Davey's life as he watched Dale Jarrett win the Winston Cup Championship that Davey opened the door to many years ago.

Margie Lambert

A Champion's Reward

In early 1998, I went to my first NASCAR race to humor my Dad. He loved car racing, and had been a Mark Martin fan for as long as any of us could remember. As he hoped, that first race proved to be just the first of many as I was hooked from the thunder of the revving engines. We watched in anticipation, my Dad on his feet, as Mark Martin lead the race. My Dad, not who I would typically think of as a zealous fan, was practically leaping in the air as the checkered flag flew. I remember being grateful that Mark Martin won that race at Las Vegas because I wasn't sure I could stand to see my dad cry.

In July 1998, my dad was diagnosed with cancer. The statistics were dismal and chances of survival slim. My dad faced several grueling weeklong chemotherapy treatments in the hospital and permanent damage from intensive radiation. Right away my family rallied around Dad and the hero we thought of for inspiration was Mark Martin. Not only was my dad one of Mark's biggest fans, but also we admired Mark's ability to triumph over his personal difficulties and continue racing even after a family crisis such as the death of his father.

We told the doctors that Dad had to be home by Saturday morning so he could watch the Busch races and Winston Cup races from the comfort of his own bed. We brought framed Mark Martin posters with inspirational sayings to hang in my Dad's hospital room. As far as we were concerned, every race Mark Martin won that year was a race for my Dad.

My Dad made it through the treatment but had lost

60 lbs and was extremely weak. At almost 6 foot and less than 120 pounds, my Dad was grateful to be alive, but barely strong enough to enjoy it.

We began plans for Las Vegas, this time with the hope that my Dad would be well enough and strong enough to make it. Being a computer oriented family, we were used to using the web to find out information about the next NASCAR events. I happened upon a charity auction that had been announced at the last minute, which would benefit Speedway Children's Charities, and decided to attend.

The evening was exciting, watching fans bid on the drivers they cheered for every Sunday. Everyone was intoxicated with the possibility of meeting their favorite drivers and riding the parade lap on Sunday. It seemed like the evening went on forever until the auctioneer got to Mark Martin. I was sure that the price would go so high that it would be out of reach. But because Mark was so late in the evening, the fans had spent their money. I was so excited to bid I could barely keep my paddle on the table. There were three of us bidding, each nudging up the bid a little more. Finally, with the thrill of victory, the auctioneer declared that Mark Martin was "sold." It took me a moment to realize that I was the winning bidder!

I spent all the rest of that night trying to decide how to tell my dad. I wanted it to be "perfect." The next night, when my family arrived, we went out to dinner. I started casually telling Dad about the auction and told him how excited I was about meeting Robin Williams. Then I told him that he was going to be even more excited when he got to meet Mark Martin. My dad, a very calm and business-like person, was stunned. He jumped out of his chair, his body animated in excitement, his eyes full of tears. I told him that after having been through the horrific cancer treatments of the last several months, we thought he deserved something a little more fun. We were tickled when Dad immediately started worrying about what he was going to wear, what he was going to say to Mark Martin, all the kinds of things we never expected from Dad... it was wonderful. We teased him that as long as he didn't call Mark Martin "Jeff" he ought to be okay.

That Sunday morning, my dad was weak in physical strength, but strong with joy and excitement. He couldn't sleep the night before, he wasn't interested in breakfast, and he was impatient to get to the racetrack.

The opening ceremonies seemed to take forever. We could hardly wait for the driver introductions. My brother and I kept getting in trouble with the track officials as we tried to get closer for good pictures. In exasperation, one of the officials finally agreed to use my camera and take pictures. I don't remember the race starting, I only remember waiting for Dad to get back to the seats after that parade lap. We watched him struggle to make it up those steep stairs, obviously exhausted. I don't remember who won in 1999 at Las Vegas, but I will never forget the grin that lit up Dad's face. After months of watching him suffer and his spirit struggle to survive, Mark Martin had given us all the gift of a dream come true for my dad. My dad, my childhood hero, had gotten to meet his hero.

Ginger Wolfson

An Amazing Lady

I've been a NASCAR fan all my life. My dad was a driver in the late '40's and early '50's. He was the 1950 Modified champion. He died in Virginia at the young age of 43, when I was only 10 years old. Being a driver was his job, and in that time and place it was difficult to make ends meet as a driver. To say that I understand the sport, perhaps more than most, is an understatement.

My husband and I attend at least six Winston Cup races each year, along with three Busch races. We attend both races at Pocono, as it is only a short distance from our home. We have been fortunate to witness many exciting events, and feel lucky to be a part of racing.

In 1998, we were lucky to be at the Pocono race and witness Jeremy Mayfield win his first Cup race. I was very excited for both Jeremy and his crew. After the race, while gathering our belongings and heading off to the car for our picnic supper, I decided to stop at the ladies room. Of course, there was a line and, as is my usual habit, I began to talk with the other ladies. In particular, I spoke with the woman directly in front of me in the line. I thought I recognized her, but wasn't sure. I didn't want to make a fool of myself. When she turned completely around, I noticed her NASCAR license and realized that this was indeed Thelma Kulwicki, mother of Alan Kulwicki. I told her how much I admired her late son and that, even though I'm a die-hard Bill Elliott fan, I was thrilled that I was in Atlanta to witness him winning the Championship. I also mentioned to her that I was happy for Paul Andrews, who had been Alan's crew chief, and that day was Jeremy's crew chief. At that point in our conversation, she reached into her pocket and pulled out a card. On the front was a picture of Alan with Davey Allison at the 1992 Awards Banquet, and on the back were the words, "Champions Forever!" I thanked her for her kindness and we each proceeded to our stalls, where the sound of gentle weeping could be heard from both of us.

Susan Tribucher

Love and Inspiration

During my younger years I was like most teenagers, footloose and fancy-free. I didn't care much about anything but boys, clothes, music, and cars. I remember every Sunday my father would sit in front of the television watching racing. As I breezed in and out of the house you could hear him get excited, but I never paid much attention. Once in a while I would sit down with him for about five or ten minutes and ask him what was going on. He would say, "You won't believe what that Dale Earnhardt just did. That boy don't take nothin'! I tell ya' he's something." This Sunday activity had been a ritual in our house from my earliest remembrance.

When I was 18 I got married to a man I had loved for two years with all my heart. Our first child came later the same year. The early parts of our marriage were rough. We were both still very young, he was only 20, and now we had a new baby. We hadn't gotten a real chance to learn to be together as a married couple before we became parents. We had a really hard time getting along, but all I knew was that I loved him. We struggled through the first few years and had another child. We were having a hard time finding anything that we had in common other than our children. I guess we were both determined to stay married because we really loved each other. I would frequently get depressed because we rarely had money to do anything. My husband was a homebody and I was the type to mingle. He always won the argument about going out, so we stayed home most of the time. I didn't have any hobbies or close friends and this added to my depression.

Nine years into our marriage I went outside one day to find my husband listening to a NASCAR Winston Cup Race on the radio. He loved to stay outside and piddle around while I stayed inside. I told him, "If you like racing, let's see if it's on television." I thought "What the heck! My dad always loved racing and if my husband likes it, we'll watch it together."

We went inside and found the race was on. My husband said, "Okay, pick a car, pick your driver." I sat there for a while watching the cars go around and I finally said, "I like the guy in the black car. I'll take the black car with the number three." Little did I know that was the same car and driver my husband liked. We had such a good time watching that race and cheering for Dale Earnhardt. It became something we enjoyed together. Watching Dale race did so much for me. Watching his antics and his iron man attitude were truly exciting. I always did like real gutsy men with a bad boy attitude.

NASCAR Winston Cup racing has completely changed the relationship between my husband and me. We finally have something in common other than our children. We talk about racing and Dale Earnhardt all the time and keep up with everything that goes on in the sport. We never miss a race and we are enjoying our fifteenth year of marriage, now with three children. We go to at least two to three races a year together in a used RV we bought from a friend. We look forward to each and every one and are proud to have Dale Earnhart's flag waving from our RV. Everything is better between us and we now have a good time together doing everything. We have one son racing go-carts now and talk about someday when our children are older maybe moving to North

Carolina and working for the sport. We have already bought property up there. NASCAR Racing and Dale Earnhardt have been a very inspirational part of my life and the lives of my children. I only wish I had stopped on occasion and really sat down to watch a race with my father, who continues to do so to this day. Maybe I would have seen all the things Dale did in his career and been a 15-year Earnhardt fan by now.

Thanks NASCAR!

DW from SC

Change of Heart

My brother and I are die-hard Dale Earnhardt fans who manage to get together once a year for a NASCAR race. He lives in Huntersville, North Carolina, and I live in the Poconos of Pennsylvania. Along with many other fans who were pulling for their favorite drivers, we often complained about Jeff Gordon's dominance of the sport. During the 1999 season, I was invited to the Pocono International Raceway for the time trials of the Pennsylvania 500 as a guest of Pepsi Cola. (The primary sponsor for Jeff Gordon's Busch Team was Pepsi Cola.) The day was to include a picnic in the Chalet Village with Jeff Gordon. The invitation stated, "The official soft drink of Pocono Raceway invites you to meet Jeff Gordon." The itinerary stated that there would be a question and answer segment, followed by pictures and autographs. I decided that even though I was not a Jeff Gordon fan, this was a once in a lifetime opportunity.

As my wife and I drove to the racetrack, we joked about all the nasty things we had ever said about Jeff Gordon and his team. I was looking forward to sending a picture of myself with Jeff to my brother with the caption, "Jeff Gordon fan for life."

The weather was great that evening as we enjoyed watching the time trails. Afterwards, we went to the Chalet Village for our picnic. As we were eating our meal, Jeff arrived at the pavilion. After a short introduction, Jeff was answering questions like a public relations expert with 20 years of experience. He continued answering questions for over an hour and then he began to sign autographs and have his picture taken. My wife and I got in line to meet Jeff and to get his autograph. She was first to get Jeff's autograph and have her picture taken with him.

I told my brother later how I had handed my wife the camera as I approached Jeff with my newly purchased Star Wars/Pepsi die cast #24 Busch car. As Jeff autographed my car, he was very standoffish. He talked down to me in a very conceited tone of voice as he asked me how long I had been a fan of his. I began to give him my answer as my wife was snapping the picture. I told him point blank that I had never been and would never be a Jeff Gordon fan. I told him that I was a Dale Earnhardt fan. As he gave me a very puzzled look, I told him, "Hey, a free meal is a free meal. Anytime it happens to be at the track, all the better." I had only hoped to be able to sell the die cast car he signed for twice what I had paid for it at the NASCAR store. Then my bubble burst and the earth stopped rotating as my wife told me that she had to retake the picture because my eyes had closed when she took the first one. She instructed me to get back down on my knee so she could retake the picture. Of course, I was extremely embarrassed; however, I knelt down next to Jeff as my wife took the second picture. One week later I picked up our pictures from the local drug store. The best picture was the one taken of Jeff Gordon and me immediately after I told him I was a Dale Earnhardt fan and was only there for the free food. As my wife took the second photo, Jeff put "rabbit ears" behind my head. I sent the photo to my brother in Huntersville, North Carolina. We had a great time with the picture, as well as my fabricated story.

The truth was that Jeff was extremely down to

earth and had spent twice the allotted time that he was obligated to for answering questions and signing autographs. When it had been my turn for an autograph, I asked him if he had a sense of humor. He proved that he did when he agreed to put the rabbit ears behind my head as my wife took the picture. He laughed and played along as we told him of our plan to fool my brother. I learned that not only did Jeff have a great sense of humor, but also that he was the perfect ambassador for NASCAR. As we drove home, I told my wife that I will continue to cheer for Earnhardt, but I will no longer "boo" Gordon.

Richard Rabenold

Kindness in the Face of Adversity

It's usually the same routine day in and day out as I board aircraft and send people on their way. But the day John Andretti boarded my plane, I knew it was going to be different. I remember saying to him, "I wish the whole pit crew were here!" He laughed in agreement and took his seat. The flight was going to be delayed for maintenance so, when I finished my work, I told him how much I love NASCAR and asked if he would mind talking to me for a while. He said he didn't mind at all and we talked for nearly an hour.

We talked about everything from rules to drivers. Throughout the conversation, he never lost interest and he made me feel as though we had been friends for years. He shared stories with me about his experiences and I shared mine with him. He even teased me about my NASCAR collection and said it would be gone when I married. After all the talking, it was finally time to go. Before he left the plane, he stopped to see me again, signing some autographs and taking some pictures with me.

This experience may not sound very unique, but when I went home that night, I looked up the NASCAR website and found that John's grandfather had just passed away. I was heartsick and felt such sadness for his loss. Then, it hit me. I sent this great man to his grandfather's funeral and he still took the time to talk to me and make me feel special. I wondered if he talked to me out of appreciation for a fan or if it made him feel better to take his mind off his loss. I like to think it was a little of both.

I've never had anyone take me aside and make me

feel like such a friend upon first meeting him, but John Andretti did. Someday, I want to thank John for the special moments he spent with me on that airplane and for all the enjoyment he gives us weekend after weekend on the racetrack.

Thank you, John, and know that you really are appreciated!

William Kirk II

Rusty's Bolt

My brother, Jerry, along with many others in Rusty Wallace's native home of St. Louis, is a huge Rusty Wallace fan. As a gift to him, my brother-in-law, James, once stood in line for over an hour to get an autograph from Rusty to take back home to Jerry. My brother proudly displayed the photo in his NASCAR theme recreation room. On a vacation to visit me in Charlotte, North Carolina, James happened upon an unexpected Rusty Wallace souvenir to take back home to Jerry.

As a real estate broker, I frequently am asked by clients to maneuver my vehicle into places I would rather not, but the customer is always right. This concession has caused me to pick up many unwanted nails and bolts in my tires over the years. While showing a client homes around the Lake Norman area, just north of Charlotte, we came upon the construction site for Rusty Wallace's new home on the lake. My client wanted to sneak a peak at the work in progress and I reluctantly pulled up onto the site. The building supervisor came out and asked if he could help us. When we inquired if he would be willing to let us tour the home, he explained that they had to say no because so many fans had come onto the site and taken things away as souvenirs. Security had become extremely tight. I turned my vehicle around, but not before picking up a huge bolt in my tire.

When I returned home, I told my brother-in-law about the incident. A mischievous grin came over his face as he immediately set to work plugging my tire for me, extracting the offending intrusion. He came into the house and asked for a zip lock bag to put it in.

"Why would you want to keep that thing?" I asked.

"The last time I got Jerry a Rusty Wallace souvenir, I had to stand in line for an hour. This little gem only took me about 20 minutes to get!" he explained, holding it up like a trophy.

James took the bolt home to Jerry, detailing the circumstances under which he had acquired it. Jerry proudly displays it, alongside the treasured picture of Rusty. "One man's trash is another man's treasure," but who could have known the value of a "Rusty" bolt?

Jan Teel

I Am A NASCAR Fan

Here I sit, 51 years old, having been born with NASCAR. I saw my first race at the age of three, now it is up to 190 races. Yes, I am a "NASCAR FAN." When I was a small boy, I would sit in our old car next to my dad as we listened intently to the race. Fireball passed Lee, or Junior passed Buck. It was great. I even went with my dad to several races.

In 1965, I got my driver's license, after which I could drive myself to the sport that seemed to be a secret kept from everyone but southerners. I went to the first Rockingham race in '65 and watched with beaming eyes as Curtis Turner made his ban from racing pay off with a win. In 1966, I went to six races. My passion kept growing until I found myself going to every race within 100 miles, and there were many back then. By the '70's, I was closing in on my 100th race. I had been a fan of several drivers up until that point. Entering the 80's, I found myself attending races for the race and not the man driving a certain car. I had become a "NASCAR FAN." I liked every single driver out there, even if they had never won. I knew there was something special about them all--their courage, desire and will to run it into the corner wide open. Whatever it was, I was hooked.

I worked for a short while with a NASCAR team, just enough to teach me the things I needed to know about the sport I had come to love so well. After learning about the cars, I decided I needed to know more about the men in the machines. In 1985, NASCAR started The Winston. I've been to most of them. When they started the Winston Cup Preview, I went to those as well. I have over 300 autographs. I live close to the heart of racing in Charlotte, North Carolina. My dad worked for the DeWitt family and I have had access to the shops of Benny Parsons, who is still a friend of mine. His championship crew chief, Tex Powell, had a shop a couple of miles away. I get my NASCAR knowledge by going to Tex Racing, or to Ellerbe, North Carolina to see Benny Parsons. Entering the '90's, I had close to 150 races under my belt. All the ticket stubs and programs were still in my possession.

Entering Y2K NASCAR, I find myself unable to choose a favorite driver. To me, the car that takes the checkered flag Is the best that day. I see people leave the races in droves if their driver has problems and is no longer in contention. That's not for me. I will stay long after the race is over. I can't seem to get enough. I've never been a rich man. I wouldn't know what to do if I was, but I find enough money to get me to the sport I grew up with. You don't hear me complaining about the prices. I will go if I have to save for months. Yes, I am a "NASCAR FAN." I will always and forever be grateful to the men and women of the sport that was meant for me. I intend to see at least 200 live races. I also intend to be a fan of all drivers. To me everything else in sports is just a game. It is my hope that maybe more NASCAR fans will surface and stand up and cheer for all the drivers. They need it so badly. I never boo anyone. I never hold anything against any of them, and I cry when we lose one of them. There can only be one explanation for a man like me. I am Walter Mabe, "NASCAR FAN," awaiting my next race.

Walter Mabe

CHAPTER SEVEN
Memories

"You can overcome anything in the world but fate."
Richard Petty

Trey and Tia

I'll never forget that race as long as I live. It was Dover, in June of 1995. It was my birthday and I was looking at the clouds all around. I don't know why I talked to Tia, maybe because she always used to get what she wanted from me. I said, "Tia, go find Trey and go find God. I know you can hear me, so please let us run good today. We don't have to win, but we have to run good. I'm having a hard time today and it's not for my birthday, it's for you and I love you." When that race started we couldn't lose.

Ever since I got that call on November 26, 1994, my life changed drastically. It was all a blur, but about 5:00 a.m. we got a call and the voice on the other end of the line said, "You've got to get down here." They didn't tell me I had lost my 17-year-old boy, Trey, but they told me my 16-year-old daughter, Tia, was gone. Another child was gone, too. Only two of the five children had survived a crash with a drunk driver as they were coming home from a party.

A lot of people say you learn how to deal with it. I think you search for a way to deal with it but you never find it. I didn't want to race at all. I didn't know what I wanted to do. It hurt so bad I didn't want to get out of bed. Nothing could ever hurt me as bad and I think about it every day. I could have turned into a bum, but they wouldn't want me to quit. That's the one reason I'm still doing it.

It's very seldom you find a teenager who spends half his summer with his grandparents, but that's what my little boy did. He'd drive up and spend the week at the race with me and then go and spend two weeks with my mother and father up in Winston-Salem.

That's just unheard of in this day and age. That's the kind of spirit Trey had. He was a great athlete and a great student. He pitched a no hitter his junior year and had some colleges looking at him. He wanted to go to Wake Forest University and play baseball. He was very good at basketball, but he chose to give baseball 100 percent. He was worried that I wouldn't like that because of how much I love college basketball. He asked me one day, "Daddy, would you mind if I concentrate more on baseball? I feel I could do a better job with it."

I said, "No, but thank you for taking that approach and caring about my feelings."

His team was picked to win the state championship until he died and then they fell to next to last out of eight teams. That next year all the moms, dads, and the kids in the dugout said they felt Trey's presence during their games. They called him their guardian angel. They would get behind in games and they always found a way to come back and win them. When they would score, the people in the stands started chanting "Trey! Trey! Trey!" They became the champions that year thanks to their guardian angel. Rather than finish next to last, where they were picked, they won the South Carolina state championship. I'm as proud of that as our Winston Cup Championship.

An incredible thing happened at the kid's funeral. First, I became a Christian, and then Max Helton, the Chaplain of the Motor Racing Outreach, looked around and there were a whole lot of hands raised and ready to come forward and commit their lives to the Lord that day. That was something that he has never done at a funeral in all his years of ministering. Then

Tia and Trey's local preacher told the group something I didn't even know. Trey and Tia had become Christians about a month earlier. When I learned that, I felt a lot of the pain go away. I know it wasn't forced on them because my wife, Jan, and I didn't know about it. I didn't even know they were attending a church. I thought to myself, "I'm going through the toughest day of my life, but God is good." Max told me something I've used to help others going through the pain of loss. He said, "Do you realize that your worst day was their happiest day?" I hadn't thought about it, but it took a lot of the burden of grief off of me.

There was a time when I wasn't a very good person. I wasn't saved, but this loss changed me. I think God is using me as an example to others who are having a difficult time, and it doesn't have to be with death. A lot of people see me because I'm in the public eye a lot and they say, "He's doing a pretty good job." Whether I am or not, if I can help one family out through difficult times, be it financial, trouble with their loved ones, or death, I think that's my reason to be in earth. I mean, I have won over 100 races. I've won a Championship. I have nothing to prove in this Winston cup. I'm back here because that's where my friends are.

We have set up scholarships at Wake Forest University in the memory of Trey and Tia. Two years ago Trey's scholarship went to a varsity basketball player. It was nice to turn on the TV and see a player in Division One going to North Carolina and winning the NIT tournament for them. Tia's scholarship always goes to a cheerleader. They compete for it. Tia had been an all-star cheerleader herself. This year Trey's scholarship went to a baseball player. Jan was tickled because this kid took his team to the ACC Championships and they beat Florida State. The recipients come to a celebrity golf tournament we set up as a fundraiser. It is a great feeling when these kids give you hugs and tell you if it weren't for you they wouldn't get to go to these schools. How can you beat that?

I know in my heart what happened at Dover that day with Kyle Petty's victory. I had two little brothers working with me in the pit that day. I went and got them both when that race was over. We were walking to Victory Lane and I said, "I want to tell you both what happened before we get down to the Winner's Circle because it's more important." I had my eyes shut, praying to Tia to find her brother and go find God, before the race. I briefly opened my eyes and saw the clouds open and a beacon of light came down. I heard them say, "Gentlemen, start your engines!" When I opened my eyes again, those clouds closed up and I tell you we could not lose that race. We were in the longest race of the year; it was a five-hour race at Dover and we didn't make one adjustment on the car all day long. Kyle started thirty-seventh and the odds were really against us. He hadn't won in a couple of years and I hadn't won since 1990.

I believe that my children were angels. Tia knew something was going to happen before the accident. She slept with her mom all week like she was afraid, or knew she was going to die. They were kids you never had to worry about. The day of their funeral, when I found out that they had both been saved about a month prior, it really bothered me. They had gone to church on their own and I didn't know that. I wonder about it now. I knew that they were wonderful children and that's made all the difference in the world because I know where they are and I know I am going to see them again.

Barry Dodson, Max Helton, and Ron Camacho

Davey

"It began years ago when Davey was driving. I liked all of the Allison's, Davey just followed in Bobby's footsteps. He had a special place in my heart. Davey was just a real laid back, sentimental, family-oriented guy who loved everybody. If he had a good day at the track, that was great and if he had a bad day at the track, well that was OK too. He was just that good-natured and he was that good at racing too. He would have had several championships today had he lived.

"My husband, lovingly nicknamed 'Kermit,' and I moved up from Florida and bought the Texaco on Poplar Tent Road in North Carolina, not more than 10 minutes from the Charlotte Motor Speedway. In 1980, Davey, Bobby and all the drivers would stop in regularly.

"When he'd come in we just started talking. We discussed life and just about anything and everything. He would come back to the office and sit down with me and then we would go out to the picnic table out in back of the station. He would pull his hat brim down over his head. He reminded me of Beetle Bailey sitting out there. Of course, nobody knew who he was.

"We were sitting out there one day and he said, 'You know, Miss Lois, you see that butterfly, that gold and yellow Monarch butterfly, that flew by?'

"I said, 'It's beautiful!'

"He added, 'Life is too. Live it to the fullest, every day. When the butterfly starts out in its cocoon and it's struggling and struggling and struggling, and then finally it gets out, what happens to it?'

"I said, 'Well it just flies away.'

"He said, 'That's right, you see it every now and then and it's gone. That's how life is.'

"We continued to talk and that week he went on to win the first Winston under lights in Charlotte."

"With the 007 car," Kermit chimes in. "That was the most exciting Winston I have ever seen in my life. Well, Kyle and Davy were side by side at 200 mph coming across the finish line and Davey won by a nose, spun out and hit the back of the wall. They had to take the crashed car to the winner's circle because he was in the hospital. He never did get to go to the Winner's Circle. He woke up in the hospital a winner. Isn't that right, Lois?"

"That's right, Kermit. That race ended up a real shoot out with Kyle Petty. That was a big one. I still have it on tape. In the wintertime, when I have withdrawal symptoms, I put my old tapes in and watch them. They had to cut him out with the Jaws of Life. Anyway, Davy won it. So that just made my day.

"I thought Davy was one of the greatest drivers that ever hit the track. I would go to the racetrack and I would watch one car--28. I could care less where the rest of them were. What they were doing didn't matter to me. After Davy died, I had to learn how to get back to the track. I had to train myself to watch all the cars.

"After Davey died, Brenda Barrett, the girl that runs Davey's souvenir rig, called me from Talladega. She said, 'The strangest thing happened today.'

"I said, 'What was that?'

"She said, 'There was a black and gold butterfly that came in the souvenir rig and it would dart from here to there.' It is unusual for a butterfly to get in a crowd--believe me, there is always a crowd at Talladega. She just thought it was a little mysterious.

"I said, 'It was probably Davy, just checking up on you.'

"About a week later I'm on the register at the store and this man came in with a Havoline hat on. Right on top of his Havoline brim sat a black and gold butterfly. I said 'Oh my gosh!'

"He said, 'What's the matter ma'am? Do you feel alright?'

"And I said 'Oh no, it's a butterfly.'

"He said, 'Well it won't hurt you.'

"I said, 'Well, I know that.' He turned and the butterfly flew off. So I'm yelling at Donna, my girl in the kitchen, to come chase this butterfly and it flew up on to a wall where a banner of Davey's hung; right on the name Davey.

"A few months after Davey had died, Steve Rose, the track photographer who grew up with Bobby and Davey, went to the memorial that they built for Davey. He called me and said he was going to take some pictures for me. I said 'Oh that would be great, Steve. Thanks a lot.'

"Then about a week later he called me and he sounded concerned, 'I was really disappointed in the picture I took at the memorial.'

"I said, 'Why? Didn't it come out? You're supposed to be one of the best photographers out there.'

"He said, 'No, it did come out, but sitting right on the 'D' is a black and gold butterfly. You know I didn't even see it when I was focusing. It wasn't there.'

"I said, 'Bring me the picture Steve.' So until this day, I have the picture of that memorial and of the black and gold Monarch butterfly, and my sweet, fond memories of Davey."

"Miss Lois," Kermit, and Ron Camacho

[Editors Note] On the day of the interview, Miss Lois and I where saying our good-byes and I was airing out my FORD Expedition when my two passengers asked me simultaneously if I had seen it. I said, "What?" They replied, "A black and gold Monarch butterfly just flew across the back seat and right past your head."

A Helping Hand

I have complete faith that the next half of Darrell's life is going to be even better than the first half because he's an incredible human being. He has such heart. One reason that Darrell has been able to enjoy the ups and downs of his career is that he has a unique way of looking at life that makes even the mundane fun. He's a silly person and it's one of those qualities that attracted me to him first and foremost. He has an amazing sense of humor with a willingness to be silly and quick witted. Plus, he's incredibly smart. You put all those things together and you have a pretty neat human being to live with.

There are some things that he's done over the years that I'm thinking, "I cannot believe I'm married to someone who does stuff like this. I am so conservative and quiet and here I am next to this guy who wears chrome driving suits and ridiculous glasses and loves to be in front of two-million people at one time and can relate to them." Like the DW Shuffle, I thought "Oh dear, why are you doing that? How do you have the nerve to do something like that?" Then, there's the other part of me that says, "Oh, I wish I had the nerve."

The wives of the drivers are not front line people and we are not performers. We have powerful faith and we are supportive. We are behind the scenes and are good at it. We are strong and flexible and we have given our hearts to NASCAR. If a man has a good family and a good marriage, it is in going to change the character of that man. It doesn't mean that you're going to win races, but I believe that it will change the heart of a driver and give them confidence in areas where they are lacking and strength in areas where they are weak. I just know there is something about family. It's the way that the Lord intended the earth to operate.

Years ago, Darrell was racing at Indianapolis Raceway Park and my sister and I were sitting in the grandstands before women were allowed close to the race cars. I didn't know a lot about the sport back then. There were two brothers racing and Darrell drove in between them. They wrecked each other and got mad at Darrell.

They stopped the race to clean up the mess and Darrell was on the front straightaway and one of the brothers got out of his car and had the handle from the jack and started banging on the top of Darrell's car. My sister says, "What are they doing to Darrell's car?"

I said, "I don't know. Putting some wedge in it, I guess." I was serious.

It occurred to me how wrong I was when my sister said, "I don't think it's a wedge Stevie. It looks a whole lot more dangerous than a wedge adjustment. Besides, do you put a wedge in a roof?"

Stevie Waltrip and Claire B. Lang

Someone I Never Knew

Adam Petty was someone that I never met, and never will meet. I saw him race in the Busch Series one time, and I was hoping to see him there again this year. I expected to watch him become a superstar in the Winston Cup Series, and he would have been huge...if only. I was very near to Adam in age, only a year or so younger. Being 18 years old made me feel invincible, like nothing could ever happen to me. All of that changed the day Adam passed away.

I had been a fan of Adam's ever since I saw him race on a cloudy October day in Tennessee. The thing that drew me to him was his smile--that trademark Petty smile. I recall sitting very high in the grandstand waiting for Adam to be introduced during driver introductions. When he finally came by, I was dazzled by his smile. From way up, I could see the shining smile on his face. He was genuinely happy to be here, honored to be starting on the front row. He was at home. My dad took a picture of him the moment he rode by on the car. Included in the picture were some of the people sitting below us. I took that picture out the day Adam died. I studied it closely and my eyes were drawn to the people in the stands. One man, in particular, had his back to the track, his back to Adam. I questioned him silently, "How could you turn away?" The night of his death, May 12, 1999, there was a severe thunderstorm with pounding rains, wind, thunder, and lightning. Amidst the chaos, I sat down to write the following tribute:

Memories

Today was no different
And the green flag soared
But, the One who waved it was the Lord.
The white flag was next, and it did flap,
As the wind picked up to signal
One last lap.
Goodbye. You were great,
Is what I wanted to say.
If only I had known that you would die today.
I loved your smile,
And the glow in your eyes.
Oh, it's only the good who is young when he dies.
And you were the best, or could have been,
If only time the Lord would send.
But time is up, Adam, it's time to go,
Savor the speed for soon you will slow.
You will fly into heaven, your home,
But Lee is there, you won't be alone.
I see the checkered, you're the first one by,
Godspeed you to heaven.
I love you. Goodbye.

Before Adam, I took each day for granted, living only for myself. I looked forward to the future, making plans for tomorrow, next week, two years from now. I never thought about today. I missed the beauty of sunshine, of cooling rains, and the outdoors. I took joy out of future plans, not from the present life I had been given. I realize now how many days that I have truly wasted. So today I want to live. I want to enjoy waking up in the morning, loving to eat breakfast and take my vitamins. I want to drink all my milk until the glass is empty. I want to enjoy locking the door, because it means I have my own key. I want to drive to work or school and make believe that I'm a racecar driver, within the speed limit, of course. I want to say, "Good morning. How are you?" and really mean it, smiling all the while, like Adam would have done. I want everyone to see the glow in my eyes, in my life, and in my living. I want to open the mailbox and be happy that there is mail, even if it's another credit card bill. I want to come home at night and recognize how lucky I am to have a family to come home to. I want to enjoy an evening meal with my parents and hear about how they are doing, realizing that they won't be here forever and showing them my love today while I still can. I want to read my Bible, say my prayers, and drift into a gentle sleep. I want to start all over again. I want my "I wants" to become "I will." Something good did come from Adam Petty's death, and that's my attitude. You could never imagine how much you affect other people. And all of this from someone I never knew.

Jenni Thompson

The Song

Reporters first heard of the song when some fans played it for them on a well-worn cassette tape. It was obvious the tape was not first generation. It had been passed on like the wind, blowing from fan to fan through campgrounds adjacent to racetracks all over the country.

At post-race get-togethers, the story would start, which usually led to the playing of the tape, which always led to an argument about its possible origin. Just hearing it produced the kind of healthy discussion that unites friends of the sport from both sides of the Mason-Dixon. The recording, as well as the controversy over the identity of the voice on it, spread like wildfire in racing circles.

The tape carries the musical message of a young, male singer delivering a song in a sweet and clear voice supported by what sounds to be a professional back-up band. Legend has it that the voice singing on the tape is that of racer Davey Allison, the 1987 Winston Cup Rookie of the Year who won 19 races, including the 1992 Daytona 500, before being killed at age 32 on July 13, 1993 in a tragic helicopter crash at Talladega Superspeedway.

Fans insist he laid down the track just before his untimely death. It's called "Come Sunday, I'll be Racin' For the Lord," and hearing it will make the hair on the back of your neck stand up. You'll never convince fans who've heard it that it was sung by anyone other than Allison, in his final days as a racer. The poignant ballad's lyrics make even the most boisterous race fans reverently pause in complete silence:

"...Talladega and Pocono
Lord help me keep this race car off the wall
Down inside my very soul
Jesus Christ has control
And I know that he really cares for me.
Sunday comes, I'll be racin' for the Lord
Off the turn, down the straightaway
A Thunderbird and Amazing Grace
Sunday comes, I'll be racin' for the Lord."

No one has yet been able to verify the origin of the tape. In an effort to clear up the mystery, a reporter played it over the phone for Carrie Allison, Davey's sister, and other Allison family members. They don't recall Davey ever saying he recorded a song. Further, they don't think he could sing a lick or hold a tune and so they doubt he's the singer. But, then, they also say they can see why fans would think it is him by the voice and the song's message. No one else has stepped forward to claim they sang it.

Funny, true fans don't seem to care who really sang the song. No matter what the evidence, or lack of, they will always believe in their hearts that it was Allison, sending a message out to them that could be passed on tent to camper after he was gone. To them, when Sunday comes, Davey Allison is racin' for the Lord and that's all she wrote.

Claire B. Lang

Anyone with information about this song, please contact Ron Camacho From the Heart of Racing by calling 888-663-5796 or e-mailing www.fromtheheartof.com/racing.

What Makes a Treasure

I've been a stock car racing fan for 35 years now and being a Birmingham, Alabama native, I naturally gravitated toward members of the Alabama gang-- particularly Neil Bonnett.

Several years ago, my wife and I were visiting antique shops when I hit the "mother lode" on a bookshelf filled with old sports books. To most people, my discovery would have only seemed like junk, but to me, it was a steal! I had located From Last to First by Ned Webb. It was about Neil Bonnett's rise to stockcar racing stardom. After a little bargaining, I bought the book for $5.00. When I returned home, I read the entire book and it didn't let me down. I couldn't believe my good fortune.

The following Christmas, my wife decided to give me a very special gift. She took the book to a collectibles shop owned by Neil's daughter, Kristen, and asked if she would be so kind as to get the book autographed by Neil. Kristen was so moved by the idea that she gladly agreed. A week later, my wife returned to the store to pick up the book and, as promised, Neil had signed it. My wife left the store and walked to her car. She couldn't believe who approached her...Neil Bonnett! They struck up a conversation and he told her how thrilled he was to sign the book and that he hoped I would enjoy it. Well, it was a great surprise Christmas gift that I still enjoy to this very day.

In late January, I wrote to Neil to thank him and invite him to a museum where I worked as the business director. He had mentioned our facility on his Winner's Show on TNN and I wanted to return the favor to him for being so kind. Three weeks later, Neil was killed in a crash during practice at Daytona. It devastated me that I was never able to repay his kindness. Thank you, Neil Bonnett, for your time and for giving me a reason to tell this story. I miss you.

Larry Baldwin

CHAPTER EIGHT
The Petty Family Tradition

"I figure the greatest race driver who ever lived was Lee Petty."
Richard Petty

*"I share the title with him, but Richard Petty will always be
'The King.'"*
Dale Earnhardt

The King

When I was born, Mother and Daddy lived with my
grandmother and granddaddy. There were three
brothers and four sisters all living in the same house.
We had 12 or 14 people living over there beside the
shop. I was the littlest one, so I got all the attention.
Then my brother came along.

My uncles never came home alone. They always
brought a buddy home and Grandmother never knew
how many people she was going to have for breakfast,
dinner, or supper. We were poor, but we didn't know it
because all the neighbors were the same way. We
didn't have running water or electricity. We would go
visit my dad's mother in Greensboro and it was great.
She had running water and electricity. We'd go
through the house and turn the switches off and on
just to see it. It was a great deal to go visit
Grandmother.

My brother and I were always getting into scrapes
with each other. I've got scars all over my head and
he's got them all over his head. In our household,
there was no right or wrong in a fight. We both got in
trouble. Mother and Daddy never said, "You're to
blame," or "You're to blame." It didn't make any
difference; if they were going to spank us, we both got
it. The two of us didn't play sports together because I
was two years ahead of him in school. Our social lives
were completely different, but when we were at home,
we played together and worked together.

I played football and basketball in high school. We

grew up in a rural area and most of the guys that played ball would stay after school, practice, and then play the games. After the game, they would have to go home and plow a field or milk a cow or something. I'd go home and work on a racecar. Football was my favorite sport because I got to be a linebacker. I weighed 210 pounds, so I wasn't a small guy and, you've got to remember, that was in the mid 50's and somebody that weighed 200 pounds was a big person at that time. I played in front of these guards and most of them were about 5' 5" and weighed about 170 pounds. I'd just sort of hold them off with one arm and look around to see where to go. I was pretty fleet footed. I liked the defensive part of football, too.

My dad was pretty stern with us and he wanted to be known as "Mr. Toughguy," but he could be very compassionate when he was at home and things got tough. If he had business dealings with you and he gave you his word on something, he made sure he got it done. It didn't make a difference how much of a hardship it was on him. My brother and I learned that from him. Forget contracts, it's your word, whether you write it down or not. He taught us that you are responsible for what you say and for what you do.

Mother was a peacemaker. She tried to keep the home fires burning while Dad was out racing or doing other things. Mother really raised us when it comes right down to it. She was compassionate and tried to make things work between all of us. She was the oldest one in her family of eight and the peacemaker there, too. She had a really strong faith. If we depended on Daddy, we probably wouldn't have a lot of faith, but Mother got us off to church every Sunday morning. We went to Sunday school and church here in Level Cross. It was a little wooden church and, like everybody else, we had our special place to sit when we went in. We didn't have a place for separate Sunday school classes, so the little people would meet in this corner and the big people in that corner. If there is any faith in me, it came through Mother.

I met Linda early in my racing career. We dated a couple of years, but I was out of town a lot. One night I told her, "You know I love you and, if we are ever thinking about getting married, we need to do it now because I'm not going to have time later." She said, "Okay." We went to South Carolina and got married one night. When we came home she didn't tell anybody besides her parents that we were married, not even my parents knew. It took about three months for me to get up the money to buy her a ring. After I gave her the ring, she told everybody we were married.

The Racing Tradition

Daddy was always a mechanic. He had a bunch of trucks and would haul anything for anybody. He did a little truck farming, too, with a few things he raised, but in '49 he got his first racecar. That was when the Winston Cup first started in 1949. He had a '37 Plymouth with a straight 8 Buick motor in it. People would come from Daytona, Atlanta, and all around to race. It was big money even back then. In '49 Dad read in the paper that Bill France was having a race in Charlotte. He hung out at a service station on the south side of Greensboro with some of his buddies. One of them had a '47 or '48 Buick. It ran really fast on the road. Dad and his brother talked the guy into borrowing the thing so we could take it to Charlotte and blow everybody away.

We went over to Charlotte with the car. When we got there, we pulled into a Texaco station, put it on a lift, changed the oil, greased it and got ready to race. That's all there was, at the time, to make a racecar. Dad got about halfway through the race when the sway bar broke. The thing turned over with them, tearing off all four doors. We had to thumb a ride back with my uncle so that we could get home. Even after all that, my dad said, "You know, I think I might like this racin'." He went out and bought the smallest car he could, which was a 1949 Plymouth Coupe. It didn't even have a back seat. I think it went for $890.00 and they could win $1500.00, so it was a great deal.

I don't think that Mother thought a lot about what Daddy did when he sold his truck and trucking business and stopped farming the land. He said, "Okay, we're goin' in the racin' business." This was a new venture and he didn't know if it was going to work. The first year they only ran about eight races, but he had made the commitment. He was probably the first one to say, "I can make a living out of this if I watch what I do." It was a family business from the beginning. We didn't have help and Daddy did all the work. As long as we got enough money on Sunday to get back to the race the next week, he was happy. When we first started racing, he was not that fast. He figured out that there were 200 laps and he wanted to make it to the end of the 200 laps. If he led for 195 laps and then fell out, he wouldn't make it back to race the next week. They called him "Mr. Consistency." He might not win first, but he wound up winning more races than anybody at that time. He was always second, third, or fourth. He won enough money to get us something to eat so that we could go to the next race.

I started working on the cars when I was about 11 years old. I wasn't really interested in driving them. Daddy was running and winning races and everything was going well. I said I was happy to be working on a car and building the cars. I guess I was 18 before I even really thought about driving a racecar. I graduated high school and went to King's Business College in Greensboro. I took an eight month business course, but it took me two years to get though it. I went four months during winter and then when the '57 season started, I'd come back and start working on the racecar. Even when I went to school, I'd go during the day and work on the car at night. When we had to start going to the races, I couldn't go to school at all.

When I turned 18, I went in one day and said, "Okay, Dad, I want to drive a race car." He said, "You're too young." I told him, "Buddy Baker's driving." But he said it didn't make a difference. He told me I couldn't race until I was 21. "You'll do a lot of growing up between the years of 18 and 21," he said and he was right. I got out into the world and experienced a lot more during those years.

When I was 21, I walked in one day and said, "Okay, I'm 21." He said, "There's a car over in the corner, get it ready." That's the way we got started. It was a convertible. Dale Inman, Red Myler, and I loaded it up and headed for Columbia, South Carolina with it. I had never even made a fast lap around a racetrack in my life. I had been out lots of times, but Daddy would never let me go out and run more than 50 miles an hour. Daddy and my brother headed off for a race with the hardtops in Asheville, North Carolina and they sent us off to run a race even though I had never been in a race in my life. They threw me right out there and away I went. It took me a long time to learn to drive, but we finally brought in a winner.

My brother, Maurice, was the engine builder. He had polio when he was four years old and he was out of commission for about six months in Duke. He played a little basketball and he was a good football player because he was big and strong. In the early '60's he ran about 10 or 12 races and did pretty well. He turned a car over a couple of times in Columbia one night coming out of the second corner. He got out and said he was going home. "I'll tell you what," he said, "you drive the car and I'll work on it." I agreed. He became our official engine builder. He always said, though, "If you're going to drive the car, you need to work on it, too." So, he would work on the engines, but I'd still work on other parts of the car. That's how he became known as "Chief," because he was the chief engine man. He was good at building engines. Anyone who has built between 250 or 300 winning engines has got to be good. When you compare him against any of the other engine builders, there isn't even a second place. That's how far ahead he is of the people that build engines.

Kyle was born around 1960, right in the beginning of my racing career. Linda and I had been married a little over a year and we were living with Mother and Daddy. Kyle was born into the same house that I was born in. Linda and I saved up some money and bought a mobile home and put it in the front yard. We finally moved out into our own place, but it was really small. Within 12 months, our daughter, Sharon, came along and that place seemed to get even smaller. We didn't have air conditioning in the trailer, but we had a '60's Chrysler and it had air conditioning. We'd eat supper, put the kids in the car, and go out and ride around until they went to sleep. Then we'd come home and put them in bed.

Someone asked Kyle what it was like growing up being Richard Petty's son. He said, "I don't know, I never grew up any other way." When I was home, we did things together, playing ball or taking them to the movies. When I was on the road, Linda took care of things. In the summertime, we took the family with us everywhere. I had one of the children under each hand and Linda would have the third one, along with the diaper bags. We didn't have nannies. We put the little ones in the back seat and we went because that was our family. Nobody set standards in front of us to say, "This is the way" or "That's the way you do it." We just did it the way my mother and daddy did it.

The Fans

I was fortunate to be with the Winston Cup racing as it was growing. We were driving an offbeat car, a Plymouth. At the time, everybody else had Fords, Chevrolets, and Pontiacs. When the Ford fell out of the race, the Ford fans wouldn't pull for a Chevrolet, but they would pull for the Plymouth. The Chevrolet fans would pull for the Plymouth before pulling for the Ford, and so on. I think that we may have gotten a lot of fans because of that. We were fortunate to win 27 races in one year and people would scream for you to win more. You see very few people that really hate Richard Petty. They might not be a Richard Petty fan, but they don't down me that much either. My first race I signed one autograph, my second race I signed two. I have always looked at the fans as the guys who were paying the bills. If it weren't for the fans, I wouldn't be out there in the first place doing what I want to do. Every time I sign an autograph it's like saying, "Thank you for letting me do what I want to do and make a living out of it." The racetracks have never paid Richard Petty a penny; the sponsors have never paid me anything. The fans that have bought the tickets and the products are responsible for my making any money in this business.

The times are so much different for drivers today. There may have been only 6,000 to 10,000 people at the racetrack in the beginning. Now there are 107,000 people and there is no way that drivers can take the time to do the same things with the fans and the press that we used to do. There used to be two or three people lined up to see you, but now there are hundreds. There used to be, maybe, one sponsor, but now there are hundreds of sponsors. The racers of today do not have the time to do the things I was able to do. The one thing that I am proud of is that I did take the time to do it and a lot of the new drivers coming through say, "We have to do it now, because that is the norm." That makes me feel good.

The Accidents

Right at the time that my career was taking off, Dad's was winding down. He won the championship in '58 and '59. He was third or fourth in the points standing in '60 and then I think he won only one race in '61; then he got hurt at Daytona and that was basically the end of his career. He and Johnny Beauchamp got together right at the end of a 100-mile race and they went through the fence and turned the car over and it demolished everything. We had no sponsors on the cars at the time. We had two cars and I had just wrecked one in the first 100-mile race in corner one and he came through corner three and four and crashed the second one, so we had no racecars at all. They carried him off to the hospital with a punctured lung and a torn up knee and broken leg. He was in pretty bad shape. We went to the hospital and you could see where they had taken him because there was a trail of blood coming out of the back of the ambulance. A bunch of people came in to donate blood. For two or three days he laid there and they didn't even operate on him. They just tried to keep him alive. I went in there on Tuesday and he said, "Come here." I leaned over and he said, "You and Maurice go on home and go up to Greensboro and buy another car. Mother and me will be home about Friday." He was home on Friday--about four months later. That's how badly he was hurt, but he was ready to go. "Let's go racin' again."

I've had some bad wrecks and been beaten up pretty badly, but if I can wake up and see the ceiling, I know that it's okay. Every wreck is different. After some of the wrecks, I could remember everything that happened and with others, I could only remember part of what happened. I think that the good Lord has got a little mechanism in us that, when you get close to death, causes you not to remember. It seems like He blocks that out of your memory so that you don't wake up in the middle of the night screaming with the terror of it. The big wreck at Daytona in '88 was spectacular.

But I felt like a guardian angel said, "This going to be a bad wreck." Then he took me out of the car, turned it over and then stuck me back in. I know this has happened more than once because I've seen some of the wrecks and I say, "No way are you going to get out of there without getting hurt." I'm usually conscious of what's going on, and most of the time I can get out of the car by myself. At Daytona I remember the doctor coming to the side of the car and asking, "Are you okay?" I said, "Yea, I'm okay, I just can't see anything." I was blinded for probably five minutes, but the doctor said my sight would come back and it did. It wasn't until after I had seen the films of the accident that I knew that the car had turned over.

Linda came to the hospital and I could tell she had been crying. Once she knew everything was fine, though, she was mad. She had gotten over the hurt part and moved on to anger. All the times we talked about racing and accidents that happened, we had reached an agreement. I always told her, "When we are not having fun anymore, I'm not going to do this." She came in there gritting her teeth and said, "Are we having fun?" Everybody just broke up laughing and any hurting I had just went away.

Life Lessons

It hurts a lot more to see someone you love hurt than to be hurt yourself. When Kyle was hurt in Talledaga, Linda and I went in to see him. His bone was sticking out of his leg and I felt like we were hurting even worse than he was. I remember when Adam was driving the ASA car, early in his career, and his crew let a jack down on his crew chief. The boy

died later on. I ran into the same thing in '65 while drag racing in Georgia. Something broke off the car, causing it to run off the track where it hit and killed an eight-year-old boy. I could relate to what Adam was feeling at that time. I was a little bit older, but Adam was just 18. It wasn't his fault; he had nothing to do with it, but when you are involved you feel responsible. Adam came through that tragedy well. He had to have a little bit of faith in order to get through it. I had talked to the Chaplain at the ASA board and he had consoled Adam. When he returned home, I talked with him as well.

After Adam was killed, I was talking to the chaplain again and he said, "Adam had a lot of faith in order to overcome that." He had blamed himself to a certain extent but he said, "You know, even if I'm to blame, I'm not totally to blame and I've got to go on with life." The same is true for Kyle, Linda, Patty and myself. When Adam died, I questioned it. We got a letter from a lady right after Adam's death that said, "Never put a question mark where God has put a period." I settled right down after I heard that. I said, "Okay, I'm not going to question anymore." We have to go forward with our lives. We have 10 other grandchildren and we can try to help them. You would like to have the eleventh one here, but it's like Linda was telling someone the other day when they asked how many grandchildren we have. She said, "We have ten on earth and one in Heaven."

Richard Petty

"What lies before us and what lies behind us are tiny matters to what lies within us."—Unknown.

Kyle

Up until the time that I was eight or nine years old, I thought everyone's father had a racecar. I didn't know that anybody did anything else. I never thought of what my father did as being different from what anybody else's father did. We just went to races on the weekends and traveled around and saw a lot of the country from the time I was in the first or second grade. We went to California, New York, Florida, and a little bit of everywhere.

We used to go up and down the highway in station wagons or regular passenger cars. This was long before the minivan or big vans were around. It was nothing for us to leave on a Thursday afternoon and drive straight through to Michigan, which could take 15 or 16 hours 25 years ago. If you say, "Okay, how can families be close together?" I say, "Just lock them in a car and make them ride around for 16 hours and they'll be close." My sisters, Sharon and Lisa, would have their own little world, playing with Barbies; I'd be in the back with a baseball glove and we'd all be talking together. I think that's why we are such a close family now. We talk almost every day. I may go for two weeks and not talk to my father because he's off in California making appearances, but my sisters and my mother and I talk on a daily basis.

When anything new came along on a car, like electric windows, or lights in the back, we'd run the battery down by leaving the lights on. There's nothing my father hated worse than to come out after a race

and the battery be dead in the car. On one of our trips to Michigan, a fuse blew and we got locked in the car because we couldn't get the automatic door locks to open. My mother pulled up at a Chrysler dealership and the salesman came out to find this woman with three kids in a car screaming through the window because the window wouldn't roll down, either. They had to get a slim-jim and pop us out. The main thing that I remember about growing up were those times spent in the car, not the time we spent at home.

We grew up next door to my grandfather in a small farming community called Level Cross. What was really great about growing up around here was that everybody knew you. The guy down the road was a dairy farmer and the other direction was a tobacco farmer. To them my father wasn't Richard Petty, he was just Richard, and my grandfather was just Lee. You didn't pay any attention to what your last name was because you lived in a rural community and raised your families there. Maybe that's one reason that this place has been here for 50 years. The family farms around here have been here for 75 or 100 years.

I always compare our racing business to a family farm. For us, our farm was the racecars; it just happens to be that we have cars instead of crops. If you look around Level Cross you see where my grandfather and grandmother lived, which is where my father and my uncle were born. If you go next door to the house, there's a shed that they started the racing out of. It was out of that house and shed that my father and I raced. Several members of our family, both extended and immediate, work for Petty Enterprises. This has always been a family endeavor. When my

grandfather started, it wasn't about going out and winning the trophies; it was about putting food on the table for your family. It was about survival when they started, but this is all we know and it is all we do.

There are times when the family connection hasn't been the best thing and we've suffered tragedy because of it. From the time that my father started dating my mother, her brother, Randy, helped in the business. Uncle Randy just thought that Richard Petty hung the moon. He always wanted to work on racecars and be around them. He would work here during the summers of his junior high and high school years. Randy was only five years older than me and was more like a brother than an uncle. He went to work full-time for the business after high school. He had been working for a couple of years when a pit road accident happened in Talladega. An air tank or water tank blew up and killed him. I think that was a hard time for the whole family. Randy was my mother's only brother and to my father he was like a son. After the accident, Dad had to come back and be with my mother and my grandparents on my mother's side, and that was very hard for the family to get through.

You try not to think too much about the accidents. You knew if you drove there could be accidents, serious accidents, and people could get hurt. Not only people in the racecar get hurt, but people outside the car. I think that's been shown to us with Randy and through two or three other accidents that happened to other teams on pit road and in the garage area. You try to make some mental block in your head that says, "Yea, that could happen, but its always going to happen to somebody else." You never think about it

happening to you. When it did happen to you, you dealt with it and then you put it in some compartment in your head and your heart and went on. Some things you forgot about, but some things you didn't forget about. Some things always keep coming back, but you deal with it.

I started hanging out around the business when I was 12. From the time I was in the third grade, I went all summer long with the race team. As soon as baseball season was over, right after school was out, I would travel with my father. In my senior year of high school I told my father I wanted to drive and race. He told me I had to wait until I was 21. All my life he had said I had to be 21, but I said, "You know, I'd really like to try to drive a racecar." He said, "Well, you know your mother and I really want you to go off to college." I told him, "Just let me try it and if I don't like it, then I'll go to college." That was the kicker because I think he knew I was going to like it and he knew I'd never go to college. My mother wanted me to be a pharmacist. I can't imagine myself being pharmacists. The majority of the driving instruction I got was from my father because my grandfather had been out of the business for a while by that time. I could go and ask my father for advice and most of my help came from him.

I ran my first race when I was only 18 years old. It was the ARCA race at Daytona. I had no experience, just really good people working with me, obviously here at Petty Enterprises, and I was fortunate and won the race. I don't remember a lot about it. They give you a car and say, "Go run 195 miles an hour." You're just having a good time; it's just like going to the fair. When I look back on it, it was just a lot of fun, but it wasn't my job. My job was still working on the pit crew and

working for my father. I drove his car one week and won a race and then as soon as Monday came around, I was back at the racetrack working on his car and doing other things with him. That's the way the first two or three years went. I'd drive sometimes and I'd work on his car most of the time because I didn't have a job or I wasn't driving full time. I didn't start driving full time until about '81.

I met my wife, Patty, through my sister, Sharon. My sisters had horses and we went to a horse show where Patty was doing some things with Sharon. I found out that Patty worked for Winston and she was one of the R. J. Reynolds girls. We dated for a couple of years and then married in '79. She didn't grow up around the racing. Her father worked a regular 9 to 5 job and had weekends off and took normal vacations. I sometimes think it was hard on her in the beginning, but gradually she's gotten used to the lifestyle of racing. That has been 22 years ago in February and I still have horses. I've been trying to get rid of those horses for 22 years and I still have them. Now I have a little girl, Montgomery Lee, who's 14 and loves horses. She and Patty share their love of horses. That gives them an opportunity to go to the barn in the afternoon and hang out together. We all make fun of her because she's 14 and she spends more time with her mother than she spends with anyone else. That's an opportunity!

Our son, Austin, has always loved kids, even though he's still a kid. When he was 12, he loved the kids and babies. As he got a little older, he started spending time at camps and doing things with different church organizations. When we were in Charleston, they had a group that went to Romania to build

playgrounds and orphanages. He went with a missions group over there and spent three weeks there when he was 16. He helped to assemble prefab playgrounds and had a really good time. I think he saw a lot of the world and how blessed he was to be a part of our family--not just the immediate family, but the extended family that includes my sisters, nieces and nephews. He realized how blessed he was to live in this country. Until that time, I think he thought that every country was exactly like America. When you look at the bombed out houses and some of the pictures, you see what a stark contrast there is.

This past summer, Austin went to a camp in Florida for critically ill children as a counselor. One week they bring in kids who have aids and another week they bring in kids with cancer or hemophiliacs. This gives the kids an opportunity to be with other kids with the same disease. If you have a kid who goes to a school where he's the only one with cancer, he feels like a freak. When you give them a chance to be with other kids who are facing the same problems, they share a common bond with each other. When they come to camp and relate to each other, they are just kids for a week and they understand that they are not freaks. Austin spent three months down there this summer and he has been heavily involved in that for the last three or four years.

We always tried to spend a lot of time with our children, Adam, Austin, and Montgomery Lee. The one thing we realized early was that they were totally different people. You couldn't lump them in and say, "We're going to do this." You had to go do things Adam liked to do and then things Austin liked to do. I think that's been one thing we've tried to do with each of

them. Another thing that we've done from the beginning is to live in small houses. We never had a big house. Everybody's room was right there together. Even today, Montgomery Lee and Austin's rooms are right above us so that when they get out of bed in the middle of the night you can hear them and you know where they are and they know where you are. Every night before we go to bed we all gather in our room and say prayers and we always have. From the time that Adam was born, and from the time that each one was old enough to walk and talk and understand what prayer was, we have prayed together. Even with the recent tragedy with Adam, Montgomery Lee and Austin still come in and we all get together and say prayers before we all divide up and go to our own rooms. Austin may be gone to a movie until 11:30 or 12 o'clock at night, but when he comes in we get together. I think that's the one thing we've tried to do so that we're all in touch with each other every day at some point, even if it's only for five or six minutes.

I've always wanted to be a part of everything my kids did. I wanted to go with them and be with them no matter what they were doing. During the years my grandfather was raising a family, his main focus was keeping his family alive. He was molded and shaped by being born in the early 1900's and coming through the depression and two world wars. Society taught men that you go off to war, you fight, you come back and you don't talk about what you saw. There was no such thing as being "shell-shocked" and having "syndromes." Guys just came back and picked up and were basically expected to carry on from where they left off. My father came along and was molded, to some degree, by the changes in America during the

'50's and into the early '60's because he was a young man in the early '60's during the time of Vietnam and the civil unrest. His focus, too, was on putting food on the table for his family. When I was born, Vietnam went on, but show me a nine year old who paid any attention to Vietnam. You knew it was happening, but it didn't affect you that much. I had the luxury of being able to relate to my family in a different way than my grandfather or father could.

It's easier for fathers to show emotions to their little girls than to their sons. You know, I can't imagine not kissing Montgomery Lee or telling her I love her every time she walks out the door. At the same time, I think that's what you should do with your sons, too. Adam never got into a racecar that I didn't kiss him and say a prayer and tell him I loved him. He never walked out the door that I didn't tell him I loved him. We never hung up the phone without saying it, and the same is true with Austin. Austin never leaves to go out on a date, he never goes to bed, I never hang up the phone without telling him I love him. When Adam went to New Hampshire, the last time I talked to him on the phone, Montgomery Lee and I were on an airplane flying to England and we called him from the air. We both told him we loved him. There's not a doubt in my mind that he knew that we loved him when the accident happened. I think that the most important thing in life is to tell your kids that you love them because if you love them, they know they are loved and then they'll pass that love along to somebody else.

I always tell Austin and Montgomery Lee to just be kids while you're this age. This is the time when you're supposed to act like a kid. When you're 40 and you act

like a teenager people get mad at you. When you're 15 or 16, you're a kid and that's what you're supposed to be. There's nothing sadder for me than to see these kids that come up and become professionals when they are only 12 or 14 years old. They are athletes or movie stars and so serious about what they want to be and do; I think they've missed a big chunk of what their life should be. Adam could be a mischief-maker, but one day he woke up and he was incredibly focused. He was 16 or 17 years old and he decided he wanted to race.

I did with Adam what my father did with me--I neither encouraged nor discouraged him from pursuing racing as a career. I have steered Austin and Montgomery Lee in the same way. I tell them, "One day, you're going to wake up and decide what you want to do and what you want to be. When you're sure in your heart of hearts that's what you want to do, I'll help you any way I can. If I don't know how to, I'll call somebody and give you a leg up to get started down the road you want to go down, but I'm not going to point you down the road and say, 'Go down this road.' That's not my job." There are so many things in this world today that people can do. Do something that you enjoy doing. Racing shouldn't be about the money part of it or the glory part of it. It should be about being around racecars and racing people. Adam went down that road, but Austin couldn't really care less about the racecars. He enjoys going to races, but he doesn't want to be a racecar driver. Montgomery Lee enjoys the horses and she's dedicated to them, but that's probably not what she's going to do for the rest of her life.

Adam started by running go-carts with one of us.

Archie Kennedy, one of the guys who works for Petty Enterprises, had a go-cart and got him involved in that. Then he did some Legend stuff and one day we got a late model car. He wanted a late model stock car, so we bought it and I told him, "You put it together, we'll work on it, and we'll go racin'." We worked on it for about three weeks and then he didn't show up anymore. He just got tired of it. About six or seven months went by and one day he came back and said, "I think I'm ready to put that thing together now." We went back and worked and then he was ready to do it. It wasn't that we pushed him or didn't push him. I told him, "You never have to work on it, but you're not going to drive it unless you do put it together."

After Adam's death, we sat down and talked about who would drive the 45 car. I think we all decided that since we had some control over it, it was important for me to drive it. It has been more of a healing process to get back in the car that he was in and work with his team. In some way, you feel that connection, that closeness. Little by little, that part will go away, but at this point this is something I feel I need and my family needs. We need to see that car continue; to be able to go to the shop and see those guys working on the car has been a part of the healing process for all of us.

When I look back on the 40 years I've been alive and the things that have happened in my life, there are only really two or three defining moments that changed the course of my life and sent me in a different direction. The first one was when my Uncle Randy was killed and I was only 14 or 15. I realized that when he was killed you couldn't just take the hands of the clock and click it back and rearrange events to make it not happen. Once I do something,

there's no need to look back on it, because you can't change it. It's just gone, you've let the moment slip by and it has passed you. At the same time, in the same hour, I realized that I needed Christ as a personal Savior because there was more than just being here on earth and doing what we do and I think that was a defining moment. I went for several more years before Adam's accident and that was another defining moment. He was here one day and then he wasn't here anymore. You begin to question what is important. Winning races and all the other stuff isn't important. Montgomery Lee's important, Patty's important, Austin's important, and my relationship with Christ is important. Helping other people and making people's lives better or happier is important. We refocused on that sort of thing after the accident, supporting the Starbright Foundation that Adam had been a part of and several other children's charities.

I can look at what happened to Adam and cuss the day that I was born or cuss the day that he was born and just be very bitter about it. Instead, Patty, Montgomery Lee, Austin, and I sat down and said, "No, it was a blessing to have him for 19 years." Let's look at all the things Adam did for us and what we learned from him in that short period of time. He was not an angel, but he was a good kid. He could get his rear end on his shoulders if he didn't want to do something or he could turn around and be the nicest kid in the world. Adam had started to realize how important his spiritual growth was as he got older and was involved in the Starbright Foundation. He was aware of how incredibly blessed he was to be in the position he was in and he was just starting to take advantage of that and witness to other kids in

hospitals. I think that was becoming more and more important to him.

It is absolutely amazing how many people have lost a child. We get between 10 and 15 cards and letters every day, even though it has been six months since we lost Adam. We draw strength from others who have been through this, but the loss of a child is incredibly hard. I lost my grandfather this year and that was tough and I've lost grandparents in the past; but it's not like losing a child, whether it is a son or a daughter. It has definitely refocused me and my Christianity. To say that God gave his only Son, you can't imagine how hard that was. I've got two sons, I had Adam and I've got Austin. One of my sons is gone. I can't imagine how hard it was that His only Son was sent to save all of us. It would be an incredible sacrifice for a human, much less for a God. People say to me, "You know, it'll get easier with time." I tell them I hope it doesn't. I hope it hurts till the day I die because if it does, it'll keep me focused on where I need to be.

We are blessed that God gave us life and we should go through life loving it, enjoying it, and making the most out of everyday. We should try to help somebody along the way, too. There is a great saying I've heard two or three times that goes, "You never help somebody climb the hill without getting a little bit closer to the top yourself." I think that's the way it is. As we go through life, if we can help somebody along, the first thing you know, we're a little further down that road, too.

Kyle Petty

About Ron Camacho

Ron Camacho grew up in a small town in upstate New York and attended the Buffalo State University, majoring in art. While there, he started the "fanzine" known as the *Shakin' Street Gazette* and began his career as a music critic. His work led him to the signing of two bands with Columbia Records and he went on to become the road manager for such groups as Blood, Sweat, and Tears.

For 20 years Ron was road-manager, bodyguard and promoter, for some of the top performers in pop and rock music—including George Michael, Chaka Khan, David Lee Roth, and The Black Crowes. He eventually left rock 'n roll to pursue country music with the same passion that he had for rock. Ron set up his company, American Entertainment Concepts, in Nashville, Tennessee. He wrote, produced, promoted and marketed Chicken Soup for the Country Soul, the 16th edition in the #1 paperback around the world, proudly representing country music and its lifestyle.

Since leaving the "Soup Group" two years ago, Ron has committed his life to the From the Heart book series and his new publishing company, The Healing Voice. Future editions include, From the Heart of the American Veteran, From the Heart of Law Enforcement, From the Heart of Rock 'n Roll, a people's choice book, and From the Heart of Formula Racing and Beyond.

To contact Ron for events surrounding the book promotion, appearances, or concerts, please contact:

American Entertainment Concepts, Inc.
128 Holiday Court, Suite 116
Franklin, Tennessee 37067
Phone: (615) 599-9996 or e-mail: ron@amentco.com

About Max Helton

Max Helton is the founder and Senior Chaplain of Motor Racing Outreach (MRO), an interdenominational ministry that serves the racing community internationally. Max started MRO in 1988 in cooperation with three NASCAR drivers and their wives in response to the need for a "church" for the many families traveling and competing on the Winston Cup circuit. Today Max and 16 other full time and volunteer chaplains serve 21 racing series, "taking church to the track."

Born in Conasauga, Tennessee, Max was raised by his pastor father and was preaching at an early age. He attended Tennessee Temple University and received his Doctor of Divinity degree in 1972 from Hyles- Anderson College where he also served as Executive Vice President. He has served as pastor to several churches within the United States and in the British West Indies.

Max currently serves on the Board of Directors for MRO, Sports Outreach America and the North Carolina Museum of Auto Racing. He is listed in *Who's Who in Religion* (1993), *Who's Who in the South* (1992), and *Who's Who in the West* (1989). He is the recipient of the Mike Rich Memorial Award (1993) and the Bill France Award of Excellence (1992). In 1996 he published his first collection of daily devotions, *Beyond the Checkered Flag.*

Max and his wife, Jean, live in Huntersville, North Carolina, and have raised five daughters in their 38 years of marriage (6/8/62). They have four grandchildren. Max enjoys going where most people don't go!

Smith Tower, Suite 405
5555 Concord Parkway, North
Harrisburg, NC 28075

Motor Racing Outreach (MRO)

The mission of Motor Racing Outreach (MRO) is to introduce the racing community (racers and fans) to a personal faith in Christ, growth in Christ likeness, and active involvement in a local church, through relationships that provide care, sharing knowledge of God's word, and assistance in developing their leadership skills.

MRO is a, non-profit organization founded in 1988 when founder Max Helton was summoned by three drivers on the NASCAR Winston Cup circuit to minister in their unusual situation, as racers, and their families, are rarely able to attend "normal" church services.

Motor Racing Outreach
Smith Tower, Suite 405
5555 Concord Parkway South
Harrisburg, NC 28075
Phone: (704) 455-3828
Fax: (704) 455-5806
e-mail: info@go2mro.com

Mission Statement: Speedway Children's Charities is dedicated to helping children. We are a non-profit foundation that distributes funds to qualified children's charities. All funds must be used to directly affect children and their needs.

Speedway Children's Charities hosts a wide range of events and promotions geared around Race Weeks at Speedways and supported by teams of volunteers. Currently the staff to volunteer ratio is 1 staff member to 122 volunteers. Grant requests are accepted from non-profit organizations providing direct services to children. These requests are submitted to the chapter's Board of Trustees at the end of each year for evaluation. Each Board's objective is to assist as many children in need as possible. In 1999, the Charities awarded over 1.2 million dollars to 160 non-profit children's groups, representing an impact to more than 122,000 children in need.

We invite you to take the opportunity to learn more about Speedway Children's Charities.

National/Charlotte Office
5555 Concord Parkway Suite 336
South Smith Tower, Harrisburg NC 28075
Phone (704) 455-4396   Fax (704) 455-1099

Winston Cup Racing Wives Auxiliary

The Winston Cup Racing Wives Auxiliary, Inc. was established in 1965 as the Grand National Racing Wives Auxiliary, Inc.. While serving the needs of stock car racing families through efforts to promote better understanding and relations among its members, the Auxiliary has always had charitable work as its main goal. To accomplish its central objective, the Auxiliary immediately established a charitable Trust to receive private donations and funds from its numerous money-raising efforts.

The Auxiliary's mission statement is, "To promote the sport of stock car racing through its programs of assistance and support for all Winston Cup families. This effort includes raising funds for the Trust, which provides medical and financial help for all Winston Cup race participants suffering injury or tragedy."

The Winston Cup Racing Wives Auxiliary, Inc
5700 Concord Parkway South, Harrisburg, NC 28075
704-455-WAXX 9299) Fax: 704-455-9307

About BSLA

The Busch Series Ladies Association (BSLA) was formed at the end of the 1996-racing season by a group of women who felt that they could contribute to the well being of the families of the Busch Series. The objective of the BSLA is to promote the general welfare of the wives and families associated with the Busch Series, promote fellowship among the teams, and represent the Series and sport in a beneficial way.

The BSLA is drivers, driver's wives, driver's mothers, car owners, car owner's wives, car owner's mothers, crew members, crew member's wives, crew member's mothers, pr reps, pr reps wives, manufacturers reps, manufacturers rep's wives, media, NASCAR Officials and NASCAR Official's wives. But most of all the BSLA is a group of women who pray everyday that the Busch Series Ladies Association never has a reason to send us a check. The BSLA financially aids members of the Busch Series who receive a debilitating injury.

Contact BSLA:
Po Box 124 Davidson, NC 28036

For public relations and marketing information please contact marketing@buschladies.com

For general information please contact:
info@buschladies.com

The Boggy Creek Gang

A Hole In The Wall Gang Camp

The Boggy Creek Gang is an expansion of the original Hole In The Wall Gang Camp, located in Ashford, Connecticut. For no cost to the children or their families, this permanent, year-round center will accommodate young people with serious diseases.

Most importantly, the prescription for the day is fun, fun, fun!

Boggy Creek Gang Camp
30500 Brantley Branch Road
Eustis, FL 32736
www.boggycreek.org
352.483.4200

Collectable NASCAR Prints of Many of Your Favorite Drivers Available!

FOR A FREE CATALOG CONTACT US AT:

Visual
MARKETING
INTERNATIONAL

www.visualmarketing-nc.com
704-522-8660
1101 Tyvola Rd., Suite 201
Charlotte, NC 28217

A Made In The USA Original...
The "Anatomy of a Race Car™" Series

* Antique Finish
* Personalized
* 100% Fine Pewter
* Made in the USA
* Limited Edition
* Detailed Chassis
* Hand Welded
* Hand Finished
* Individual Serial No.'s
* 100% Satisfaction Guaranteed

Race Car Body & Chassis Approximate Weight 4 lbs.

Race Day Edition

The Race Day Edition comes with a single level display case measuring 18 ½" long, 11"wide, and 5 ½" high. Display case has clear top with mirror back and wood base has mirror floor. Display comes with a solid pewter race body with all graphics raised on surface accompanied with detailed chassis. Body and chassis are raised off floor with pewter stands for easy viewing.. Pewter medallions of the Petty Enterprises logo, Sprint® Racing logos and personalized nameplate are attached to mirror base. Centered between body and chassis are pewter accessory group of race day equipment (wheels/tires, jack, fuel cans, air guns and safety stands.)

Order Information: Race Day Edition $325 each (includes personalized nameplate)

I would like to order _____ of the #45 Adam Petty Race Day Edition

Method of Payment: VISA or MasterCard
Card # _____ Exp: _____

Shipping & Handling $14.95 each
(Continental U.S.)

To Order you may call: 1-800-260-8660
OR
You may e-mail us at: mdc@fair.net
OR
Visit our website at: www.motorsports-diecast.com

MDC
MADE IN THE USA

____ Race Day Ed. @ $325 ea. $ _____
____ S&H Chg. @ $14.95 ea. $ _____
Total: $ _____

Name: _____
Add: _____
City,St,Zip: _____
Phone: _____

Adam Petty, Petty Enterprises & Sprint, are licensed under authorization of Petty Enterprises, Randleman, NC. All other logos used under permission.

Motorsports Development Corporation
4606 Shirley Avenue Jacksonville, Florida 32210
Questions: 1-904-388-5572 Fax: 1-904-388-7701

Shamrock Sports Group. Inc.

Four Generations
America's First Four-Generation Athletic Family

presents

Celebrating 4 generations of Petty Family racing this tapestry throw pictures Lee Petty, "The King" Richard Petty, Kyle Petty, and Adam Petty. An undeniable heritage and a lasting link to the roots of NASCAR....America's Sport! Woven in 100% cotton using the finest pre-dyed colors, this tapestry throw will provide years of use in your home or as a gift for that special someone. This is a limited production item available through the Petty Museum and Shamrock Sports Group, Inc. Get yours today!

$49.99
plus S/H
VISA, MC
Allow 2-4 wks. for delivery

Available with matching 18" x 18" Tapestry Pillow

$25.99
plus S/H

Mural on both sides!
18" x 18" Tote

$23.99
plus S/H

Dowel Included
26" x 36"
Great Detail!

$39.99
plus S/H

100% cotton
Adam Petty Afghan
Approved by Petty Enterprises
All royalties to be donated to charity
53" x 67"

$49.99
plus S/H
Add matching 17" x 17" tapestry pillow
$19.99
plus S/H

100% cotton
Beautifully done with King's signature and Petty Enterprises logo against a backdrop of a multitude of the Kings silhouettes.

$49.99
plus S/H
Add matching 18" x 18" tapestry pillow
$25.99
plus S/H

Call 1-877-590-3242 To Order

for other racing home decor items

All items are available through The Petty Museum and Shamrock Sports Group

Interested Dealers Please Contact:
Shamrock Sports Group, Inc.
Monroe N.C. 28112 (704) 238-9114
FAX (704) 238-0603 • RN # 102591